Praise for *Beyond the Bond*

"*Beyond the Bond* is a courageous and compassionate reframing of what it means to be a twin in a culture that too often romanticizes sameness. Dr. Joan Friedman invites us to see twinship through a new lens—one that honors individuality, autonomy, and authentic connection. This book is more than a guide for twins and their families—it's a mirror for society, challenging us to release outdated myths and embrace the soulful complexity of human development."

—Roseanna DeMaria, Adjunct Professor, NYU School of Professional Studies, and founder of DeMaria Group

"*Beyond the Bond* is a potpourri of fascinating stories and information about twins, with something for everyone! Whether you are a twin, a parent of twins, or even a twin's teacher or caretaker, this book is filled with useful tidbits you never even knew you needed to know. It is a true treasure trove."

—Betsy Brown Braun, child development and behavior specialist, author of *Just Tell Me What to Say* and *You're Not the Boss of Me*, and mother of adult triplets

"This new book about twins and twinship by Joan Friedman is a welcome addition to the literature on twins. Based on her own practice, Friedman has clearly and succinctly illuminated the main issues confronting twins in their development and lives. It is a most readable book covering important issues."

—Vivienne Lewin, Fellow of the British Psychotherapy Foundation and author of *The Twin in the Transference* and *The Twin Enigma*

"With depth, empathy, and remarkable clarity, the author brings to light the emotional complexity of being a twin. It's an outstanding and powerful contribution—essential for twins, their families, and anyone who wants to truly understand the world of twinship in all its nuances."

—Liana Kupferman, LMFT, twin specialist

"A fascinating exploration of the twin bond and all that lies beyond it. This book of essays addresses so many of the challenges that twins experience across the lifespan, while also helping their families, educators, and professionals better understand the twin dynamic."

—Katie Wood, Associate Professor and Clinical Psychologist, Swinburne University of Technology

"Dr. Friedman sensitively and precisely addresses the central dilemmas in the lives of twins. The book highlights the wide range of challenges facing twins and their parents and provides clear examples from clinical work. A must-read for twins and their families."

—Dr. Hila Segal, mother of twins and twin researcher, Longitudinal Israeli Study of Twins

"Friedman blends research with real-life stories, capturing the beauty and challenges of twinship—from identity struggles and comparisons to the deep emotional connection that often forms between twins. It neither romanticizes nor overdramatizes the twin experience, instead presenting it with nuance and empathy."

—Maria Markodimitraki, Professor of Psychology, Department of Preschool Education, University of Crete

"Essential reading for anyone raising twins. Friedman helps parents understand the unique emotional bond of twinship and how to nurture it without losing sight of individuality."

—Stephanie Ernst, founder of TAPS Support and parent of twins

"Dr. Friedman offers compassionate, practical guidance for parents, twins, and clinicians alike. Her insights illuminate the challenges of identity formation, individuality, and emotional development within the twin bond, making this book an invaluable resource for nurturing healthy, autonomous lives."

—Emma Otta, PhD, Director, Painel USP de Gêmeos (the University of São Paulo Twin Panel)

"*Beyond the Bond* is a thoughtful and insightful guide filled with real-life stories and expert advice for anyone raising or supporting twins, triplets, or higher-order multiples. Whether you're living this experience or simply curious about the world of multiples, this is an essential and eye-opening must-read."

—Laura Pérgola, President of Fundación Multifamilias, Argentina

"*Beyond the Bond* is an invaluable and comprehensive resource for twins and their families. It is a bold, honest, and courageous look at the complexities of twinship and provides the blueprint to help twins transform limiting relational patterns and reach their full potential in life. Dr. Friedman's book is a true gift to twins and those who love them."

—Amy Tierney, LCSW, psychotherapist and twin dynamics specialist

"*Beyond the Bond* is a terrific read for twin parents of all ages! Dr. Friedman eloquently shares her personal and professional experience to help shed light on a topic not many can understand or relate to. The book will give any twin parent insights into the inner world of twin lives and parenting to better support their twins' relationship and well-being."

—Smadar Zmirin, twin specialist and antenatal, postnatal, and early childhood educator

"I am always delighted to read another of Joan Friedman's books on the difficulties of navigating twin relationships, informed by her own experience. Her books are so helpful to me in my own therapeutic work as a twin specialist here in the UK."

>—Audrey Sandbank, family psychotherapist and author of *Twins and the Family*

"In this collection of essays, Joan Friedman offers vital help to twins and their parents in examining the complexities of twinship and moving toward expressing individuality and a sense of self during the unique twin journey."

>—Dr. Elizabeth Stewart, author of *Parenting Twins*

"*Beyond the Bond* offers invaluable insight into the unique emotional landscape of twinship, providing me as a clinician with both practical strategies and a deeper ideological framework for supporting twins and their families."

>—Dr. Elaine Nabel, PsyD, psychologist

"In a conversational tone, Dr. Friedman unravels typical situations and provides approaches to problems that until now have appeared to have no solution. For those who have been wanting to understand twinship in a practical way, this book is likely to become a classic in the field."

>—Salomon Grimberg, MD, retired psychoanalyst, art critic, and author

"*Beyond the Bond* reveals how unhealthy expectations and caregiving from well-intentioned family members can have lasting effects on each of the individuals who make up the twin relationship. These stories highlight what can be done in a positive, proactive way to avoid the pitfalls of unhealthy adult twin dynamics."

>—Christine Stewart-Fitzgerald, host and producer of the *Twin Talks* podcast and mother of adolescent twins

Beyond the Bond

OTHER BOOKS BY JOAN A. FRIEDMAN, PHD

*Emotional Healthy Twins: A New Philosophy
for Parenting Two Unique Children*

*The Same but Different: How Twins Can Live, Love,
and Learn to Be Individuals*

Twins in Session: Case Histories in Treating Twinship Issues

Beyond the Bond

Insights into Navigating the Challenges of Being or Raising a Twin

JOAN A. FRIEDMAN, PHD

Rocky Pines Press

Copyright © 2025 by Joan A. Friedman

All rights reserved. No part of this publication may be reproduced, distributed, or transmitted in any form or by any means, including photocopying, recording, or other electronic or mechanical methods, without the prior written permission of the publisher, except in the case of brief quotations embodied in critical reviews and certain other noncommercial uses permitted by copyright law. For permission requests, write to the publisher, addressed "Attention: Permissions Coordinator" at the address below.

Rocky Pines Press
www.rockypinespress.com

Ordering Information
Quantity sales. Special discounts are available on quantity purchases by corporations, associations, and others. For details, contact the "Special Sales Department" at the address above.

Orders by US trade bookstores and wholesalers. Please contact BCH: (800) 431-1579 or visit www.bookch.com for details.

Printed in the United States of America

Cataloging-in-Publication Data

Names: Friedman, Joan A., author.
Title: Beyond the bond : insight into navigating the challenges of being or raising a twin / Joan A. Friedman, PhD.
Description: Includes bibliographical references and index. | Los Angeles, CA: Rocky Pines Press, 2025.
Identifiers: LCCN: 2025907150 | ISBN: 978-0-9893464-7-4
Subjects: LCSH Twins. | Twins—Psychology. | Parenting. | BISAC FAMILY & RELATIONSHIPS / General | FAMILY & RELATIONSHIPS / Parenting / General | FAMILY & RELATIONSHIPS / Siblings
Classification: LCC HQ777.35 .F75 2025 | DDC 649/.143—dc23

First Edition
29 28 27 26 25   10 9 8 7 6 5 4 3 2 1

Disclaimer: This publication contains the opinions and ideas of its author. It is intended to provide helpful and informative material on the subject matter covered. It is sold with the understanding that the author and publisher are not engaged in rendering professional services in the book. If the reader requires expert assistance or counseling is needed, the services of a professional should be sought. Every attempt has been made to present accurate and timely information. Nothing contained herein should constitute an absolute with regard to this subject matter or be considered a substitute for legal, medical, or psychological advice. The author and publisher assume neither liability nor responsibility to any person or entity with respect to any direct or indirect loss or damage caused, or alleged to be caused, by the information contained herein, or for errors, omissions, inaccuracies, or any other inconsistency within these pages, or for unintentional slights against people or organizations.

The names and any identifying details of people associated with events described in this book have been changed. Any similarity to actual persons is coincidental.

To my numerous grandchildren
whose unique personalities inspire curiosity,
spontaneity, playfulness, excitement, and tenderness.

Contents

Preface		ix
Introduction		1
Part I	Parenting Twins	3
Part II	Parenting Adolescent Twins	29
Part III	Caretaking Behaviors	45
Part IV	Young Adult Twins	65
Part V	Romantic and Marital Relationships Involving Twins	87
Part VI	Older Adult Twins	107
Part VII	Twin Loss and Estrangement	133
Conclusion		157
Index		160
About the Author		163

Preface

THE SUBJECT OF TWINS is a large part of my life: I am a twin, I am the mother of twins, and I specialize in twin issues in my psychotherapy practice. I am also the author of three books on the subject: *Emotionally Healthy Twins*, *The Same but Different*, and *Twins in Session*.

I decided to compile this book of essays in response to the many readers of my blog—both parents of twins and twins themselves—who have told me how much they appreciate finally finding a place where their twinship questions and dilemmas are addressed by a professional who understands what they're going through. Parents of twins say that my advice to other parents helps them navigate the various stages of their own same-age children's development. I am honored to provide information for parents seeking to make healthy decisions for their twins. I also appreciate the opportunity to provide adult twins a space to understand and accept why being a twin is sometimes challenging and painful—and to help them repair and improve their relationships with their sibling, spouse, partner, and others.

So much of my own story has been built on the lessons I learned growing up as a twin. My relationship with my identical twin sister was somewhat fretful and difficult—but not to the outside world or our family. Others did not notice how both of us rushed to open our birthday presents because the slower twin would have the surprise spoiled since we always received identical gifts. They did not understand why it might have been important to sing "Happy Birthday" twice and for each of us to have our own cake and candles. They did not recognize that our terrible physical fights reflected the tension we lived with. They did not realize that having our own rooms might have been important to having space away from each other.

We dressed alike until we were ten years old; I am not certain why it took us so long to change this, other than enjoying the perks of being a twin. Looking alike lent us an air of specialness and celebrityhood. We reaped the benefits of social capital. Others flocked to us, eager to get to know the twins; however, we did not learn how to make friends on our own. As adolescence approached, we had a need to be known rather than noticed. However, since we shared the same friend group and had little or no outside one-on-one relationships, our sameness and identicality locked us into a suffocating trap that we hoped would end by attending different universities.

My sister had a beautiful transition, while I did not for many complicated reasons. She made friends easily; I felt lost in intense depressive and anxious feelings. We both graduated from college and went on to graduate school. Then we were confronted with the death of our mother, which affected us both in very different ways.

Life transitioned gradually to marriage and children. During these years we had a series of disruptions in our connection. We had different values and ideas about fundamental issues and as yet had not developed sufficient maturity and separateness to accept these differences rather than see them as cracks in our connection. Both of us felt deeply hurt and abandoned by the other whenever these ruptures occurred and had little awareness about why or how they kept happening.

I believe that struggling to find my sense of self and establishing a separate identity has been the cornerstone of my emotional health. I have been able to experience a new connection with my twin sister. I understand most of the troubling issues that adults confront through my own experience. Helping others has immeasurably helped me through rough times too. Now, in the face of our aging, my sister and I have let go of our previous rivalries and jealousies and have come to a shared place of peace and spontaneity. It does feel as if an earlier part of our twinship has been rekindled.

We feel an authenticity that had been hidden or not revealed for many years. We are no longer caught up in comparisons between our lives; rather, we laugh at our precarious predicaments without judgment or competition. We have gotten to the point where our differences are notable, defined, and recognized. In prior years, recognizing our differences might have led to disagreements or bickering about the notion that only one of us can be right. Now we commiserate about our shared health concerns and exchange stories about our children and grandchildren. A beautiful ease and serenity accompanies this feeling of connection and love without the aforementioned difficulties and conflicts that had habitually marked our time together.

Helping twins find themselves after growing up in a twinship is an arduous journey. Yet the joys and the returns are priceless. Recapturing twin magic after years of loss and despair is undeniably a dream come true.

I have dedicated my professional life to extending a helping hand to those responsible for raising twins as well as treating twins who are troubled and upset about certain aspects of their twinship. I am forever grateful for all the support and trust I have received over the years. My most important message is this: twins may have expectable difficulties growing up; however, they can develop the tools and understanding to enjoy a healthy connection.

Introduction

WELCOME TO *BEYOND THE BOND*, a compilation of my essays on all things twins: parenting twins, being a twin, and understanding the unique practical and psychological concerns inherent in a twin relationship.

I began writing about twins more than two decades ago. When I mention to people that my focus is helping twins who are having difficulty getting along, the most common reaction is surprise and disbelief. How could twins possibly have issues? Nontwins and twins alike idealize the twin bond, which is the subject of tremendous envy. Many people long for a double. They want to have a soul mate, to experience twin telepathy, and to never feel alone or abandoned.

These stereotypic and societal views influence how twins are perceived and treated. Nonetheless, the dynamics inside the twin bubble burst when the twin attachment can no longer sustain itself. Depending on the ages and developmental stages of the twins, a variety of struggles can surface, much to the surprise and dismay of parents and the twins themselves.

What is it like growing up with a same-age sibling? How do twins survive years of being dependent, compared, and competitive? Can they individuate successfully to make their own friends, live on their own, and maintain relationships outside of the twin bond? Do they learn how to negotiate conflict and accept differences? *Beyond the Bond* addresses these questions and many more.

Beyond the Bond also fulfills the ongoing need to push back against stereotypic cultural expectations and beliefs about being a twin and provides an accessible resource for understanding twin psychology from a developmental perspective.

Our Western mindset rewards individualism and self-reliance. However, many twins have been denied opportunities to develop these traits because they have been treated as a unit for most of their lives. Frequently, psychotherapy provides the safest place to explore the twin dynamics that have prevented and inhibited healthier emotional outcomes.

Whether you are a twin or the parent, grandparent, or partner or spouse of a twin, this book will provide information and support as you confront the unique challenges of twinship. Although many of the essays are about specific situations and clients—whose names have been changed to protect their privacy—my hope is that you will find meaningful advice, emotional validation, and psychological insight that you can use to understand and improve your relationship with the twin in your life.

Part I

PARENTING TWINS

MOST OF US APPROACH parenting with a mixture of joy, worry, expectation, self-doubt, and exhilaration. As we strive to nurture, guide, and support our children, we find ourselves in the ongoing process of attuning to their emotional and physical development, wondering whether we correctly understand what they're going through, what they need, and how best to teach and help them. Are we parenting too much or too little? Will our unintentional parenting "mistakes" have grave repercussions? If we're working parents, will our kids have a stronger connection to the stay-at-home parent or caregiver than to us? Is the love we have for our children reflected in our treatment of them?

With twins, parenting worries and joys are magnified, as is the challenging job of caring for two same-age babies, toddlers, and school-age children in tandem. And parents of twins are confronted early on with unique parenting concerns: overseeing the twins' relationship to each other; treating twins equally—or not; ensuring that family, friends, and teachers consider the children as individuals rather than "the twins"; deciding whether school-age twins should be in the same classroom; understanding and dealing with twins' hyper-competitive tendencies; and coming to terms with twins parenting each other or becoming locked into caretaker and cared-for roles.

The essays in this section address common parenting issues—from pregnancy through twins' preadolescence—that have been raised by my clients and subscribers and about which I offer my professional insight and advice. I emphasize each twin's need for one-on-one time with a parent and suggest how to organize consistent alone time with each twin even when it seems impossible. I'll explain why parents need to treat each twin as an individual and provide examples from my online parenting chats as well as my private practice. Readers will learn how to encourage young twins to make separate friendships and why that's important for their development, why it's okay for one twin to succeed at something when the other doesn't, and how parents can help struggling twins shine in their own right. Those who are perplexed as to why their twins are constantly fighting when they were such perfect playmates at a younger age will hear about why such conflicts are often a metaphor for too much togetherness.

I hope the advice I offer in this section will point parents toward the helpful answers they seek.

Surviving the Twin Postpartum Vortex

RECENTLY I CONSULTED with two mothers of twins seeking help to understand why they have felt persistent guilt since the birth of their twins a few years ago. In both of these cases, the birth of twins was spontaneous and natural—with no fertility issues. Initially, neither of these moms relished the idea of having twins. Both felt robbed of the traditional rituals and experiences that normally accompany the birth of a singleton. One mom was enormously disappointed that her longings for a vaginal birth were frustrated when the obstetrician informed her that a C-section was imperative given the position of both babies. Moreover, after the birth of the babies at thirty-seven weeks, she was not emotionally prepared for their weeklong stay in the neonatal intensive care unit.

As we spoke together about these experiences, it became clear to both of us that her gnawing feelings of self-condemnation and inadequacy were directly related to her inability to give herself permission to feel anger and sadness about how much the twin birth had disturbed and disrupted her romantic expectations about motherhood. She had no one with whom she could share these expectable ambivalent feelings.

Sadly, twin moms often do not have access to others that can empathize with the enormity of their situation while understanding that these feelings have nothing to do with not loving or wanting their children. Twin moms need this specific support to trust that negative emotions associated with adjusting to motherhood do *not* erase or minimize the love and concern they have for their babies.

Another mom spoke to me about feeling depressed and disconnected since the birth of her twins. She shared a harrowing story of having to spend months on bed rest in the hospital until she gave birth to her healthy twins. She had been told that it was of the utmost importance to stay positive during the hospital stay because becoming upset might induce contractions. She had never had the opportunity to understand the emotional impact of this experience. I explained that if traumatic feelings from past experiences are not revisited, often we dissociate. In other words, we push aside or forget threatening thoughts because thinking about them feels enormously uncomfortable. However, the price we pay for protecting ourselves in this way is often a self-destructive and depressive quality that interferes with our feeling connected and adequate. In many cases excessive guilt covers up unconscious or conscious feelings of anger and sadness.

I want to quote a few passages from a chapter written by a British psychoanalyst named Dana Birksted-Breen published in a book entitled *Spilt Milk: Perinatal Loss and Breakdown*, edited by Joan Raphael-Leff. She writes:

> "Postnatal blues" . . . relates to a state of mind surrounding a physically and emotionally taxing major event, particularly if it took place in unfamiliar surroundings and in an atmosphere of emergency, leading to feelings of relief, exhaustion, heightened sensitivity to circumstances, disorientation, etc. . . . Women who coped well with the experience of having a baby tended to modify their idea of what a mother should be like from an idealized one to a more

realistic one. Postnatally, a good mother was now felt to need, for instance, to be diligent, hard-working, reliable, and to like being at home with children. The women who did not cope well, on the other hand, retained an image of a good mother as "loving," "patient," "unselfish," "never losing their temper," and they felt themselves to be at odds with this image of the perfect, selfless mother.

Moms of multiples require and deserve a safe haven to express the trials and tribulations involved in surviving those early years with twins.

Dissociation during Pregnancy

AFTER I FINISHED SPEAKING to a group of mothers of twins, a woman approached me and told me about her pregnancy. Her six-month-old fraternal twin sons were doing well. She carried them to full term and had no birth complications other than the planned Cesarean birth.

This young mother needed to talk about how she felt detached from the babies when they were in utero. She said that she never really felt connected to the babies when she was pregnant. She felt bad when she heard other pregnant mothers of twins express indescribable feelings of rapture and joy about the two lives growing inside of them. She said she was happy but never felt anything remotely close to the happiness that other expectant moms felt. I explained that for some reason she was dissociated during the pregnancy—she had little access to an emotional self. Dissociation often occurs in response to a trauma, whereby we simply do not allow ourselves to be in touch with fear, grief, or anxiety triggered by an event or a series of events.

When I asked this mother about her attachment history, she described a horrific experience growing up with an alcoholic father and an unstable stepfather. I reassured her that the fear that her pregnancy would trigger unmanageable feelings likely prevented her from feeling attached to the babies. Even after her sons were born, she was mentally happy, but she felt no happiness in her body.

This mother seems to have regained full access to her feeling states and has evolved into a caring, loving, and connected mother. Just as children develop in a nonlinear fashion, so too young mothers evolve into the maternal role—in their own time and their own fashion. Be careful not to compare or be competitive. Motherhood is a very individualized journey.

Buying Gifts for Twins: Should We Give Our Twins Identical Presents?

MANY PARENTS OF TWINS ask me about buying gifts for birthdays and other special occasions. They want to ensure that they treat their twins fairly and let both children know they are loved equally. Buying identical gifts may seem like the perfect way to do this, but parents should realize that their attempt to be equalizers may send twins unrealistic or unhealthy messages. Most of us naturally give our nontwin children presents that reflect their talents, skills, and interests—but in our pursuit for perfect balance for our twins, we may not think to follow the same philosophy and buy a different gift for each twin that reflects each one's individual predilections.

Putting special care into gift giving reflects a desire to encourage twins to enjoy their uniqueness. We know that, just like snowflakes, no two people are the same. Choosing individualized gifts for our twins tells them that, even if they look very similar, we don't expect them to be the same, and we understand that they are two distinct people whose differences we want to celebrate.

For twin infants up to two years old, consider buying different variations in the same category of gift—for example, two different stuffed animals, like a teddy bear and a plush rabbit. Keep in mind that the two stuffed animals should be of equal size, however, so each child is reassured that both presents are of equal value.

In the toddler years, you can begin differentiating the gifts so they match each twin's interests and personality. But again, size is important because twins will instinctively compare their presents. Books that reflect each child's interests would be wonderful presents—say, one book about dinosaurs and another about trains. The keys are noticing what attracts your twins' attention, recognizing the differences in what fascinates them as they explore the world, and buying a gift for each that complements his or her particular interests. The more you do this, the better you know each child and the qualities that make them individuals.

Three- and four-year-old twins have a more defined idea of what they like. By this age, children have developed strong preferences for specific items. Some may be drawn to television and video characters; others may be enthralled with dolls and action figures. This is the best stage to begin buying from two different gift categories, but be prepared for the fallout that may occur.

Parents should not be surprised if one twin is not happy with his gift. Perhaps he won't get what he wanted, or he will want what his sibling received while the other child is content with his present. One twin may try to take the coveted gift away from the other to assuage his frustration.

Not getting upset if your multiples are disappointed with their gifts is vital. Try not to feel guilty or self-deprecating if you don't "get it right." In fact, if you've never bought different gifts for your twins, encountering resistance and negativity the first few times you introduce this new practice is expected. The best response is to say in a calm, soothing voice, "I'm sorry that one of you is disappointed. I did the best I could. I really thought you'd enjoy this gift. I hope I do better next time. I wanted each of you to have your own present."

Equally vital is not insisting that the contented twin share his gift with the discontented one. Each child should handle the situation in his own way. The twins will decide between themselves how they want to address this perceived imbalance.

Instead of attempting to avoid this scenario by giving identical gifts, remember that you are sending an important message to twins about life. Multiples who are always treated the same often go through life expecting that they must maintain equality between themselves. This unspoken pact interferes with their freedom to be separate. The societal expectation of equality and sameness needs to be discussed between twins and their families and replaced by the concept of multiples as individuals.

Parents of twins have enough challenges with raising two children of exactly the same age without taking on the additional burden of making each twin feel exactly the same. Parents can't make their children's lives the same; they can't even make their kids exactly equal. What they can do is encourage both children, at every age, to develop their own uniqueness.

The long-range goal as a parent is to view buying different gifts for your multiples as one of many ways to give yourself and your twins the freedom to appreciate their differences.

Powering Down the Power of Two

RAISING TWO OR MORE children at a time is a tough gig, especially if they are your first children. Parenting is an acquired skill—the more you do it, the more confident you feel making decisions and choices. Learning how to manage multiples' needs and behaviors can be a trying situation, especially if you are uncomfortable or unaccustomed to setting limits and being consistent.

Recently, I spoke to a mom of three-year-old twins who was on the verge of emotional collapse. She was doing her utmost to keep things together but was struggling with her "gang of two." Each girl was endlessly competing for the same two cookies, the same number of times on her lap, the same amount of juice in her cup, and on and on and on. When things were not to their liking, they screamed and threw tantrums until they got what they wanted. As you can imagine, the whole family was miserable—mother, father, and daughters. Interestingly, outside of the home, in structured settings such as preschool and daycare, there were very few incidents, and the girls were well behaved and respectful.

This mom, by nature, did not have an assertive personality. She tried her best to set limits but could not follow through when the girls screamed or protested. She said that she tried doing a modified reward system; however, the girls would not cooperate and destroyed the chart and the stickers.

We both concluded that the girls were anxious and upset because they did not feel secure and safe. Children thrive with appropriate limit setting because it enables them to trust the notion that adults are in control and will help them contain their messy and untamed energies. If this mother had given birth to a singleton as a first-time parent, I imagine she would have felt masterful and in charge. She is a sensitive and caring woman who finds herself in a situation that she is ill equipped to manage. I am confident that once she recognizes how much happier the family will be with appropriate limits and boundaries set, she will feel the tension and chaos dissipate.

Parenting and personality types are closely connected. Some people prefer parenting a child who is just like them or, conversely, completely unlike them. The important piece to keep in mind when parenting twins is our role in helping them appreciate their uniqueness and individuality.

Young Twins
Making Friends

MOST PARENTS ARE captivated by their twins' connection to each other. In fact, this twin bond often helps to compensate for the many difficulties and challenges that parents face when raising twins—the constant fighting, the ongoing competition for time and attention, the never-ending complaints about who has what. The wonderful aspects of the twin bond can be seen often while watching twins play. Seeing the creative and imaginative content that emerges out of their twin synchrony can be impressive and seductive. The level of comfort, understanding, and ease with which they move seamlessly can be inspiring to witness and can make parents want to nurture that connection.

Some twin pairs who spend lots of time together with little opportunity to be with other children might find it challenging at first to make friends with other children. They become accustomed to the nonverbal ease of their twin connection. They have not had to develop patience or tolerance for other children's styles of participation or cooperation. From an outsider's perspective, it may seem cruel or insensitive to hint at the possibility that the twin bond can at times be crippling or stifling. The twins may protest that they not be interfered with because they have become accustomed to being together without interference or intrusion. They are happily engaged in their twin-shared world until some conflict emerges. Astonishingly, as quickly as the conflict erupts, the reconciliation has happened.

A mother of kindergarten-age identical twin girls was lamenting the fact that her girls were slow to make friends with their classmates. Although both are in different classes, they appear less motivated to branch out. She has noticed that when they do have separate play dates, they are more engaged with the playmate's toys than with the other child. Her twins seem detached and disinterested unless they are involved in some creative play with each other.

Research bears out that identical twin girls develop the strongest attachments, so the path toward separateness needs to be slow and steady. I reminded this mom that each child develops her social skills in her own time.

Moreover, it makes absolute sense that at this age her girls are happiest playing with one another. They enjoy a synchrony and sophistication that cannot be duplicated as yet with a same-age peer. By putting each daughter in her own class, this mom has made the decision to help her twins gradually separate from each other without creating overwhelming resentment and fear. As they mature, both girls will be more comfortable moving away from each other but also will have the sanctuary of their attachment to return to when they want it or need it.

One daughter has made a friend in her class, while the other is still a bit hesitant to reach out. When the more tentative daughter found out that her twin's friend would not be in school that day, she remarked to her mom that her sister might have a hard day because of her friend being absent. Her mom noticed that the statement was made with a combined mix of empathy and scorn—a remarkably healthy dose of ambivalence. This mom understands that the twin bond is vital and nurturing; nonetheless, she also realizes that over-idealizing the relationship is damaging for both girls' burgeoning separateness. When other parents ask her why she has separated the girls, she attempts to explain their being together too much is not always wonderful—especially in the long run.

Tips for a Smooth Transition Back to School

GETTING BACK INTO the school routine after a more relaxed summer timetable can be challenging for both parents and kids. While many moms and dads look forward to having more structured time for their multiples, the school year demands that the whole family get back into a more rigid schedule—which has its pluses and minuses.

If your multiples are beginning kindergarten, this is an exciting and memorable time that requires a bit more focus and attention to the emotional details that accompany this momentous developmental milestone. As many parents of multiples are well aware, different school districts have varying policies about the placement of multiples. Some have strict regulations about separating them, and others will leave it up to the discretion of the family.

The first order of business is to find out what your school district's policies are ahead of time so that you can amply prepare your children—especially if they have not had opportunities to be separated. It's important to understand that the separation anxiety some twins experience is not so much about missing their sibling; rather, it has much more to do with the fact that they are dependent on one another to feel secure and safe because they spend so much time together. Having their "security blanket" wrested away without explanation or preparation will naturally be traumatic and scary.

So with these ideas in mind, I want to share some advice and suggestions to help facilitate these back-to-school experiences and make them more enjoyable for your family.

Dress Your Multiples Differently

Whether your multiples are in the same classroom or separate ones, it will be very helpful to dress them differently or have distinguishing characteristics that make each one clearly identifiable, especially with identical twins. Without this distinction, teachers and other children will have a very hard time deciphering who is who. At times the default position is simply to refer to each child as "the twins." Multiples want and need others to know their names; after the novelty of the confusion has worn off, many multiples feel frustrated and annoyed that they are not recognized singularly. Help them select different backpacks and lunch containers so that they feel special about their own belongings.

Educate Teachers about the Multiples' Connection

Many educators perceive the twin relationship with preconceived notions and perceptions that cloud their capacities to evaluate each multiple as an individual. My sons' high school counselor always was annoyed with me when I followed up to make sure that Jonny and David were in different classes. She told me that since twins are supposed to be best friends, she did not understand my concerns about my wanting them to have separate experiences. Be vigilant about making sure that the teacher understands your children's different personalities and temperaments and is able to recognize each one by name.

Don't Introduce Yourself as the Mother or Father of Twins

Introduce yourself as the mother of Jonny and David, for example—not the twins. You might be surprised to learn some parents of singletons have issues with twins in general—not specifically yours. They believe that twins do not want or need play dates because the twins have each other. They are concerned about having two children over and may not make an effort to get to know you. In the course of the relationship, you can make it clear that your twins would enjoy separate play dates because they are individuals as well as twins.

Watch Out for the Caretaking Syndrome

It's entirely probable that one twin may have an easier time adjusting to the new school environment. While it is important that they have empathy for one another, it does not mean that the twin who is adjusting more quickly is responsible for helping his sibling feel more comfortable. The quickly adjusting twin may not want to be in a caretaking role after having the opportunity to experience being on his own. Parenting is an adult's job, not the job of one's twin.

Be Prepared for the Inevitable Comparisons and Disparities

It is just a matter of time until one child comes home and begins to talk about how he has a friend at school, how she has made a terrific project, or how great his teacher is. This is a trying but important time for everyone to begin adjusting to a world where things are different, unequal, or unfair.

Can Your Twin Have a "Normal" Childhood If Her Twin Has Special Needs?

A MOM RECENTLY WROTE this about managing twins with different abilities:

> I have identical boys, but one will never be able to do everything his brother can, due to a complication in the womb. Although both are healthy, bright kids, their physical accomplishments will always be at a different pace, and as a result, I've had to mull this over many times.

Thinking about this mom's situation led me to learn more about how children with normal functioning may be adversely impacted by growing up with a sibling who is compromised, either emotionally or physically. Reading Jeanne Safer's *The Normal One: Life with a Difficult or Damaged Sibling* helped tremendously. I believe that what I am about to write may be construed as controversial, insensitive, and decisively not politically correct. However, I am of the opinion that an unaffected twin may be at risk for developing emotional difficulties when her twin's special needs dictate the family's psychological organization. Often "normal" children are given short shrift in terms of time, understanding, and opportunities to be authentic and honest about the difficulties of being raised with a sibling with special needs.

I grew up with an older cousin who lived nearby, and I witnessed secondhand how her mental illness affected her siblings and family. Her siblings were covertly coerced into being good girls so that their parents would not have any additional burdens or worries. Their own needs were invisible to themselves. These younger daughters had to be the children who made up for their older sister's deficits and for shattered parental dreams. They were not able to act out as adolescents or be naughty little girls. They did not dare generate any more guilt and blame for their parents, who suffered mightily with their eldest child's self-destructive behavior, depression, and psychosis.

Safer highlights the challenges faced by siblings of children with special needs:

- Maturity beyond their years
- Fear of becoming sick
- Tremendous feelings of guilt and anger
- The need to be perfect to make up for the family's struggle and loss of perfection

So often, children who have grown up with special-needs siblings go into the helping professions. Their needs are met by helping others. They watch their parents struggle and suffer and do not make demands. In a twin relationship, the unaffected twin may feel that competition is unhealthy and that her successes are not praiseworthy. She may struggle with the envy of her affected sibling, feeling as if her hard-won gains are destructive and undeserved.

Conventional wisdom says that the sooner the compromised sibling's condition is explained and understood, the easier it will be for her twin to feel less disturbed by the situation. Since the survivor guilt is fierce, however, parents must take great pains to help the healthy child realize that she had nothing to do with what happened. Parents need to reassure her that no one can undo an accident of fate and misfortune.

Since twin relationships are prototypes of future peer connections, romantic interests, and professional connections, it is vital that we help nonaffected twins develop feelings of love and caring for their twin that do not become intertwined with self-sacrifice or self-destructive motives or choices.

Separation, Not Severance

I FEEL COMPELLED to write because I am outraged, saddened, but not surprised about society's disingenuous beliefs about the "twin mystique." A recent experience recounted by an acquaintance of mine has riled my discontent. A conscientious and psychologically sophisticated mom of four-year-old twins decided to separate her fraternal twin daughters into their own classrooms. They had been together the first year of preschool, and both mother and the teachers agreed that the girls would thrive in separate classes. One child has an independent, outgoing, and free-spirited personality; her sister has a propensity to be dependent, clinging, and easily frustrated.

The mother consulted with friends, family, and professionals to discuss her concerns and ideas. Her fraternal twin sisters validated her decision; they were understanding and steadfastly supportive about their nieces needing opportunities and permission to be on their own. Understandably the mom was upset and worried when the class roster arrived. She realized that one twin would be in a class with all her friends while her sister would be in a classroom without any former classmates.

The mother attended a school event prior to the preschool's opening day. Unsuspectingly, she found herself barraged and assailed by other families about her decision to put her girls in separate classrooms. They treated her as if she were committing a despicable crime. Her sole allies were the teachers, who encouraged her to follow through with her plans.

The transition has been a bit difficult—however, not impossible, not tragic, and not traumatizing. Many developmental milestones involve a brief period of dysregulation. The twin in the classroom without her own friends does feel lonesome, upset, and envious that her sister is comfortable and happy. She cried about this with her mom and dad and told them how she felt. However, when her dad asked her if she wanted to be in the classroom with her sister, she resolutely answered no. Her parents empathically support her desire to be on her own and recognize that she has emotional hurdles to overcome.

The family feels confident that this is the right move for their free-spirited daughter. With their love and support, I am quite convinced that this child will manage the challenges and emerge from the experience feeling masterful, confident, and self-assured.

For those of you who might feel that it is wrong, unnecessary, or even unconscionable to "put a child through this" and believe that twin separation and individuation issues at this age are exaggerated or unimportant, please reflect on the following. Many of our children's expectations about their burgeoning individuation are inextricably linked to parental consideration of separateness. Do not delude yourselves into believing that the older the twins get, the easier it becomes to individuate. While in some instances this is true, in other cases it is not. Just recently I received the following email from a distraught parent:

> My twins just started kindergarten and are having an extremely difficult time making friends. For all the reasons you lay out, we have been the beneficiaries of having children whose best friend is each other. However, now we see the

harm that may have been done, as each girl has no interest in making friends and moreover does not know how to make a friend.

I can assure you that if you have faith in your child's capacity to handle age-appropriate challenges, rationally assessing whether or not your twins will benefit from separate classrooms is not inhumane, insane, or insignificant. Stereotypic as well as mythic beliefs that relationships between twins will be harmed rather than strengthened by thoughtful opportunities for alone time deserve an educated, calm, and thoughtful reappraisal by families, school administrators, and society at large. Generally speaking, it is an uninformed public that perpetuates narrow-minded thinking about twins and their needs for togetherness. What is not appreciated is that twins need advocates and parents who understand that most of us need to experience our singular shining moments undiluted by the presence of another.

Decision-Making and Differentiation

A MOM OF NINE-YEAR-OLD identical twin girls asked me to help her understand a specific dynamic that is playing out between her daughters. On the surface, the circumstances make little sense to her. Both girls take piano lessons—Annie loves the piano and practices without being asked, but her sister, Amy, rarely practices and asks her parents about playing the trumpet. Their mom understands their differences and does not make a big deal about their divergent likes and dislikes. What she can't make sense of is why Amy gets angry when Annie practices the piano simply because she enjoys the activity. The same thing happens with bike riding. Annie likes to ride her bike, and Amy is less than enthusiastic. Nonetheless, Amy gets grumpy and annoyed when Annie rides her bike outside, even though Amy has little desire to do the same.

I believe you have to be an identical twin girl to make sense of this behavior. By drawing on my own experience, I can speculate about what might be happening. While twins covet personal recognition, their differences may also make them feel uncomfortable or wrong. The notion that her sister may like something different than she does can make a twin feel angry and insecure because this palpable divergence can engender anxiety. While Amy does not like the piano, the fact that Annie loves to play may upset her because it highlights a real difference between the two of them.

Amy is not just jealous of Annie's affinity for the piano; she's likely also annoyed because this difference between them makes Amy feel that something may be wrong with her not liking to play the piano or ride bikes. Since the twins have very contrasting feelings, Amy resents Annie for making her feel as if her inherent likes and dislikes are wrong or bad. The issue is not about feeling physically abandoned by her twin, as one might assume. Rather, the issue is the complicated emotional twin dynamic that makes her think that if she doesn't like what her sister likes, something may be wrong with her ability to trust her decision-making capabilities. In other words, can she trust herself to figure out how she feels without being influenced by her twin's feelings?

Although this reasoning may seem convoluted or distorted, I repeatedly see this unhealthy dynamic played out in adult twins who are inextricably enmeshed. Since they have spent their lives making joint decisions about pretty much everything, they are paralyzed and trapped in their twinship. They have never had the opportunity to recognize and appreciate their differences and move toward individuation. After being enmeshed for so long, their differences threaten their connection and undermine their trust in and loyalty to one another.

I praised Amy and Annie's mother for noticing this subtle dynamic and bringing it to my attention for further scrutiny. I told her how much it benefits twins to learn from a very young age that their differences help define them. Again, this developmental process needs to begin early. The adult twins that I see in my practice have not been able to embrace this challenge. Unfortunately, trying to make differentiation happen all at once is unrealistic. After years of being too enmeshed and denying their own needs, twin pairs in this predicament have to work out many issues to become psychologically separate. Maintaining a healthy twin connection requires keen parental attention to helping each twin own her individuality. In the long run, attunement to and support for individuation promotes a trusting, healthy twin bond.

Part II

PARENTING ADOLESCENT TWINS

A DOLESCENCE IS A TIME when it is natural for children to want to separate from their parents and begin to define themselves as individuals. Often this developmental stage is characterized by rebelliousness and "acting out" one's resistance to parental oversight. A familiar, if dramatically overstated, refrain is "She went to bed an easygoing child and woke up a monster." The truth is, the *monster* is simply in the process of becoming an adult.

Parents of twins are confronted with additional issues during their children's adolescence, as this is often the time when one or both twins want to physically and emotionally separate not only from their parents but also from their same-age sibling. One twin may decide to drastically change her looks or behavior in an attempt to experience liberation from her sister. A teenage boy who shared the love of sports with his twin brother may choose to quit the team and spend more time with his own friends.

It can be shocking for a parent whose twin sons always seemed to be best friends to hear one boy say that he hates being a twin and is sick of having to be around his brother all the time. Or when a daughter complains that she's annoyed at always having to be seen with her twin sister—that she wants to be on her own to pursue her own interests—a parent may not know how to console the twin who feels rejected by her sibling. And since romantic connections are also important for some teens, one twin having a boyfriend or girlfriend can cause the other to feel abandoned. How does a parent deal with this perfectly normal yet potentially distressing transformation?

This section includes stories from parents who are confronting the various changes in their adolescent twins' relationship to each other. As always, it's important for parents to relate to each twin as an individual, regardless of the circumstances and difficulties involved at this time in your children's lives. Perceiving your same-age sons and daughters as a sibling couple, forever bound by a mythical twinship ideal, will only make the adolescent quest for independence more difficult. Understanding and welcoming each teen's uniqueness will help them forge a healthy pathway toward the individual identities they seek.

Don't Wait—Address Twinship Issues Now

THE FOLLOWING TWO paragraphs are paraphrased portions of a session that I had with an adolescent identical twin who lives overseas. Her feelings and experiences typify developmental concerns and feelings about teenage twinships.

> I am afraid to tell my sister to leave me alone. She'll be mad at me. I don't want to hurt her feelings. Her being away last summer was so fantastic. I did not have her looking over my shoulder, invading and intruding upon me and my activities. I made friends on my own—until she returned and took them away from me. Once she enters the picture, they include her and invite her to everything. What once was exclusively mine now belongs to both of us.
>
> Teachers and other kids always gravitate toward her. She is extroverted, funny, and charming. We became co-captains of an athletic team even though she had barely participated. The coach decided on this arrangement because he favors my sister over me. She is either unaware of what is happening or purposefully trying to take away everything I have. My wishes to do things on my own are constantly sabotaged. She wants and needs to do what I do.

After listening to her struggles and complaints, I suggested attempting to schedule a conjoint session with her twin. She replied that it sounded like a good idea, and she would think about how to present this invitation to her sister. She recalled a situation she had not considered previously. She told me that a pair of twins she had known decided to go to separate schools when they were younger. She shared that she never understood how they could have made that decision, but now she knows why.

I urged her to address these issues now rather than later. As twins get older and their lives diverge and become more complicated, serious concerns arise. For example, career choices and involvements with other intimate attachments create tensions and conflicts. If the sisters are unable to accept differences and inequities, how will they be able to preserve their twin bond? They will blame each other for the difficulties, citing competitive rivalries and abject rejection. Twins of all ages need help understanding how their twin relationship can be simultaneously difficult and gratifying. Our capacity to acknowledge and accept ambivalent feelings in all our relationships is a hallmark of burgeoning emotional health.

Adolescence: A Time to Be Tough with Your Twins

PARENTS OF TWINS, especially younger twins, celebrate and romanticize the twin bond. But preoccupation with the twin bond often prevents parents from making healthy decisions for each twin. In fact, some families are so invested in the twinship that they are unable to recognize the importance of separating the twins from time to time.

When parents ask me for advice about how to help adolescent twins refrain from constant bickering, teasing, and criticism, I compare twins to an "old married couple" to describe the twin dynamic. Like old married couples, twins are very connected in all sorts of ways. Parents often witness that their twins are bickering one minute and sitting side by side playing a game or laughing together the next minute. There is a rapid switch back and forth between the twins' moods and no apparent lasting grudge.

I am not referring here to twins who might be physically abusive to one another. That is another discussion. I am referring to twins who are teasing each other—being critical of the shirt their sibling wears, complaining that the other one sneezes too much, or bemoaning that their twin is not cool. Developmentally, at this adolescent stage, the bickering will likely intensify because one twin may want more separateness, while the other resists. Parents should advise twins who complain about being embarrassed by their sibling to do something about it (e.g., change their hair, wear an earring). Twins who are looking for independence need to take responsibility for what they want.

It's important to ensure that twins spend time apart on a regular basis. One mother saw that her twins have always resisted suggestions to do separate activities, describing them as homebodies who enjoy similar hobbies and interests. They attend the same school and share the same friends. This mother realizes that her sons are habitually comfortable and content with each other and therefore don't have the motivation to do things by themselves. In spite of the external turmoil, they internally do rely on one another without any real need for outsiders.

This codependency is a red flag that needs to be addressed. Both twins say that they want to go to separate colleges, but neither is equipped to do so. Saying you want to do something is not tantamount to being prepared. These boys are not equipped because they have had no opportunities to be on their own. How will they be ready to face college by themselves?

Like an Old Married Couple

A MOM OF SIXTEEN-YEAR-OLD identical twin boys contacted me to talk about how to handle excessive bickering between her sons. She described how she has tried to manage the incessant teasing and fighting that goes on between the two of them. One will accuse the other of dressing like a geek, having a stupid sense of humor, or acting like a dork at school. The dominant twin is more likely than not to be leveling these insults at his reticent brother. This mother had some excellent suggestions to help them individuate, but neither of them followed through. For example, she suggested that they get different haircuts or that one of them get his ear pierced. Neither boy demonstrated any willingness to follow through because they unknowingly remain very connected via this repetitive competitive rant.

The mother explained that one moment her boys are screaming and yelling at one another and next they are sitting beside one another on the couch playing their favorite video game. She compared them to an old married couple—each has his own room, but they prefer being together. Unlike their older sister, who loves to be adventurous, busy, and away from the house, the boys prefer to stay home together and share their similar hobbies and interests.

When I asked this mother if her sons had ever been separated aside from different classes at school, she calmly explained that they have never wanted to be without the other. They did, however, have plans to attend different colleges. But this desire to be separated during college without any prior experiences being on their own could be quite difficult, possibly even traumatic or impossible. I suggested making some plans for the upcoming summer that necessitate the twins be separated and on their own.

Many parents of twins are not educated about the complexities of twin attachments. Some twin pairs will most likely suffer troubling anxiety and fear if they attend separate colleges without having had any prior experiences functioning on their own.

When the Bough Breaks

A CONCERNED MOTHER OF fifteen-year-old identical twins called me to ask for help regarding her daughters' social woes and difficulties.

She explained that they have no friends. Both girls feel as if they have made attempts to connect with their peers but to no avail. When they try to make separate friends, the separate friends eventually pair up with one another—leaving the twins socially isolated and together yet again.

In response to my questions about their exposure to separate activities, the mom shared that one of the girls attended a religious camp last summer for a week by herself. Her daughter returned home emotionally traumatized. Apparently, she was ostracized by the other girls and consequently felt humiliated and abandoned.

The mother attempted to put the twins in separate classes in second grade but eventually gave in to the girls' insistence that they be together. Although they have many separate classes in high school, they spend hours together practicing for cross-country and track. They train in the mornings before school and in the afternoons participate jointly on their school sports teams.

The mother and I talked a bit about how adolescents during this developmental time frame are struggling with challenges of becoming more separate and autonomous. I explained that some adolescents, seeing teen twins together all of the time, may perceive the twins' connection as strange or weird. Teenagers are struggling to find peer groups they can identify with that will make them feel grown-up and independent.

I was terribly sad to hear that the girls summarily ignored their mother's guidance about addressing their social paralysis. They told her that they like being together and that they won't break their bond for the benefit of gaining friends. Both affirmed that doing things separately for personal growth is breaking their bond, and they are unwilling to subject themselves to the possibility of more rejection and isolation.

I explained to this mother that this social dynamic is not uncommon in the relationship between identical twin girls. Their social backwardness and overreliance on their twin relationship have inhibited their learning how to manage the harsh realities of peer interactions. Attempting to inject some optimism into the situation, I brought up having the girls ponder the possibility of attending separate colleges. I am quite sure that, underlying their emotional surrender to the "twin togetherness bargain," both harbor a real desire to find out about life as a separate person.

A Twin Bond or Bondage?

PARENTS OF TWINS often remark that one twin will snitch on the other—informing their mom and dad, reliably or not, about what his twin is up to. For instance, an incident may have occurred on the playground that the other sibling witnessed or participated in. Either way, knowing exactly what occurred and to whom is often challenging for parents.

Later on, as twins reach adolescence, they often become either partners in crime or informants on one another. Parents are put in a difficult position. While they relish being in the know, at the same time, they are jeopardizing their relationship with the nontattling twin. Moreover, these dynamics impact the twins' relationship as well. It can be devasting to realize that one's trustworthy twin has defected to the parental enemy camp.

I spoke briefly with a mom of adolescent identical twin boys who are trying to navigate this slippery slope. She described one of her sons as more of a rule follower and her other son as more of a risktaker and free spirit. The free-spirited son has told his mom that he hates being a twin. He assures her that this has nothing to do with not loving his brother. In fact, the twins are close. However, his dilemma is that he cannot be his own person. Couple this with the fact that most people cannot distinguish him from his brother, and he feels frustrated that he cannot freely act in accordance with his own wishes. First, he worries that his actions may reflect poorly on his twin since practically everyone views the pair as one person. Second, he often feels that his brother is closely watching him and preventing him from engaging in behaviors that his twin frowns upon.

This youngster seems imprisoned within his twinship due to his worries about alienating his brother. Sadly, his wish to strike out on his own is thwarted. Often, these unarticulated feelings unknowingly lead to conflict that results in twins harboring excessive resentment toward one another. This teen's perspicacity in acknowledging the effects of the twin dynamics rather than demonizing his brother demonstrates remarkable insight.

Love Me, Love Me Not

A MOTHER OF FIFTEEN-YEAR-OLD fraternal twin girls came to see me because she was concerned that the verbal and physical fighting between her daughters had escalated to a frightening degree. She told me that Elsa and Avery have always been close. She described Elsa as the easygoing twin who has habitually complied with and tolerated the overbearing behavior of her sister, Avery. But the girls' attitudes and roles have shifted within the last few months. Avery has become increasingly hostile, screaming that she cannot stand to be seen with Elsa or even be associated with her. Their arguments have become vicious and mean. Elsa has responded to this shift in their relationship by taking matters into her own hands. She has been attempting to carve out a new identity that excludes her sister and epitomizes how she wants to be seen and noticed. She has left the peer group she shared with Avery and has started dating. Despite Avery's outright rejection of Elsa, Avery resents that Elsa's boyfriend interferes with the girls' being together.

Understandably, the twins' mother is at a loss trying to understand and manage these conflicting behaviors: How can Avery be so rejecting of Elsa and at the same time resentful that Elsa is not available to her? Well, as I tried to explain, "It's a twin thing." Adolescent twins fight each other in their efforts to forge their own sense of self, albeit the modus operandi appears misguided and maladaptive.

Their mother told me that her daughters have never been separated from each other for longer than a sleepover. I suggested that possibly separating them for a week or two next summer might be a good idea.

Neither one knows how it feels to be on her own; both girls are terrified, ill equipped, and anxious. The girls are at a developmental stage whereby they are fighting to establish their individuality and self-definition, so arranging for some separate experiences would be advantageous for them.

Be Nice, Be Kind, Beware

A MOTHER OF SEVENTEEN-YEAR-OLD identical twin girls recently contacted me for advice about helping her daughters rebound from repeated social calamities. She described a pattern that started when the twins were in the ninth grade: the girls would be happily accepted by a social group, then inexplicably excluded. Sometimes they were given a lame explanation; but for the most part, the rejection seemed swift and unexpected. Naturally, both girls were upset and puzzled about why this keeps happening to them.

I spoke with both twins together. They describe themselves as incredibly nice and giving, always looking out for others' needs and making sure that no one feels excluded. Both girls shared stories that demonstrated their immense kindness and thoughtfulness. One mentioned that she always tries to be there for a friend, sometimes listening endlessly to a girlfriend's personal woes. Her sister shared that she almost missed an online exam to care for a friend.

Both viewed themselves as individuals who care deeply about others and strive to exhibit caring and helpful behavior in every possible way. So one can imagine how shocked and devasted they felt after they found out that they were abandoned by girls they considered good friends.

Of course, this same dynamic can and does play out for singletons. However, I believe examining this issue from a twinship perspective is important. I have written extensively about how caretaking behaviors inevitably evolve within twin relationships. While these habits work beautifully for many twin pairs, they can wreak havoc on other twin bonds as well as individuals outside the twinship. I can attest that the caretaking dynamic is so endemic to twins that it can become their subjective reality. They are encouraged by their families, friends, and society at large to be best friends and soul mates. How many opportunities do they have to emerge from this bubble and experience friendship in a different context?

The advice I hoped to impart to these young women is similar to what I have told other twin pairs. Being *too* nice is a trait often devalued by others. Instead of viewing the sisters' generous behaviors as positive, I suspect that those so-called friends had little respect for the twins. Many people think that "kindness overkill" demonstrates a lack of boundaries and self-esteem. In other words, the inability to assert one's own needs and be selfish alerts others to the possibility that one will not stand up for oneself.

I believe these young women have little understanding about such issues because they grew up expecting the same reciprocity in their friendships that they experienced in their twinship. Moreover, they were conditioned to avoid conflict in favor of maintaining sibling harmony. However, the sad and evident truth is that friendships usually do not mimic twinships. Friendships need to be cultivated among individuals who can be authentic, assertive, and reciprocal. If twins assume that mutuality is built into all relationships, they may be caught unaware and consequently mistreated, rejected, and sometimes manipulated by unenlightened people. Parents will hopefully stay alert for caretaking behaviors that may interfere with their twins' social experiences.

I urged both girls to make friends separately to break the cycle of sharing and losing everything.

Part III

CARETAKING BEHAVIORS

It can be difficult to reconcile that the adorable caretaking behaviors displayed by young twins may eventually transform into an unhealthy, codependent dynamic, whereby one twin feels compelled to take care of the other while the other takes for granted being automatically cared for. Both often grow to resent their respective roles, yearn to break free, but fear alienating their twin if they dare to make a change.

Some adult twins feel that they have been emotionally imprisoned in an intractable caretaker or cared-for role for most of their lives. While a multifaceted approach is needed to understand how twinship caretaking and cared-for behaviors develop, the consequences can become problematic if not addressed.

As we'll discover in the stories and advice highlighted in this section, the caretaker twin may feel worthless when her function is no longer required. Her need to be needed is so profound that without it she can feel enraged, abandoned, and betrayed. On the other hand, the cared-for twin may begin to resent the smothering, oversolicitous behaviors from her twin. Yet she may feel too guilty and fearful to reject these behaviors, worrying that to open up and be honest will upset her twin.

Often the intrusion of a third person into a codependent twinship severely tests the resilience of the sibling relationship. For example, one young man who came to me as a client never questioned his caretaking role until his brother began dating. When his brother's attention shifted to his girlfriend, my client's emotional world fell apart. His self-definition collapsed when he was no longer his brother's primary relationship and caretaker.

Such common twinship conflicts may require outside help to articulate what each sibling is going through, given that they have likely never acknowledged the caretaker dynamic or experienced being outside of it.

Twin Caretaking: Confusion and Conflict

I AM CURRENTLY WORKING with three women who are attempting to navigate the emotional turmoil wrought by their assuming a caretaking role with their identical twin sisters. The caretaker role in these instances means that one twin has sacrificed her own feelings and needs in the service of protecting and parenting her sister.

Each twin comes from a different background. Laurel was raised in a rural area by a family that was disorganized and chaotic. Charlotte grew up in a middle-class family with shifting family ties between her biological parents and stepparents. And Carolyn came from an affluent area and had overprotective and unsophisticated parents. While their socioeconomic backgrounds and emotional histories are quite divergent, all three of them struggle to understand how their caretaking role with their sister has contributed to ongoing conflict and personal heartache.

Laurel grew up amid unbearable family chaos, which consisted of physical abuse, sexual abuse, and violence related to alcohol and mental illness. Laurel is now in her midfifties and courageously coming to grips with her traumatic life experiences. She desires to develop a close and trusting relationship with her twin, whom she feels she protected all their lives against the horrific violence and abuse they both suffered. Laurel suffers from overwhelming anxiety when she feels that her sister is struggling or unhappy. Laurel is aware that she developed a defensive demeanor so as not to be overwhelmed by her feelings. Her sister tells her that she seems cold, detached, overly intellectualized, and uncaring. Since their styles of relating are so different, communicating with one another without Laurel's sister becoming angry and untrusting is nearly impossible. Laurel feels that she and her twin have to learn how to listen to one another without their protective bravado.

Charlotte is in her midforties. She is troubled because the sister she unselfishly cared for and protected all their lives becomes unpredictably critical and cruel at times. Charlotte does her best to stay in contact with her twin and relishes the times when they get along well. She is lulled into believing that the bond she has with her twin is peaceful. Then, out of the blue, Charlotte's sister becomes nasty and reactive, accusing Charlotte of not loving her and not taking care of her. To make matters worse, the sister often interferes with Charlotte's marriage in inappropriate ways that further enrage Charlotte to the point of distraction.

Carolyn is in her midthirties. She is working through an extraordinarily painful and difficult break with her sister that occurred when her twin moved away to take a better job. Carolyn's twin had always been her everything—her social buddy, her emotional anchor, and her physical security blanket. After the loss of her sister's support and her caretaking functions, Carolyn had to fight hard to come back from the loss of an identity based on her twin connection. She is working to carve out her own sense of self—a difficult task when trying to play catch-up later in life.

All three women demonstrate tremendous courage in the face of traumatic circumstances as they struggle to reclaim the individual identities that were lost in subtle twin undercurrents.

I Always Think First about What Is Best for Both of Us

Instead of thinking how lovely it is that twins care so much about each other, when I hear a sentiment such as the one above, I worry. I imagine the overly dependent relationship that most likely exists between the twins. What may begin as a compatible, caretaking, and harmonious twin attachment can turn into a relationship where one or both twins feel trapped and powerless and yet clueless and fearful about change. At some point, one twin usually desires more freedom because the burden of this ongoing interdependence with her twin becomes unbearable.

When one twin in the dyad assumes a parentified role, she becomes hypervigilant about keeping the emotional climate calm and peaceful. Usually longstanding issues of jealousy and competition have not been addressed, articulated, or expressed. The parenting caretaking twin is held hostage in this role because she feels obligated to keep her twin happy and content.

When her own needs or feelings bubble up, she hopes her sister will be sensitive and respectful to her. Unhappily, she repeatedly encounters a selfish and angry sibling who is not at all concerned with her. The cared-for twin expects that her sister will figure out what she needs and will be compliant and loving no matter how badly she behaves. In a matter of speaking, the cared-for twin emotionally blackmails her sister by refusing to go along with what she has decided is best for the pair. When her twin refuses to comply, often the parenting twin becomes anxious, distressed, and angry. She requires that her sister go along with her program so that harmony is maintained.

One young man in his late teens described to me what happens when his twin brother does not follow his agenda. When working on a joint project that requires shared participation and cooperation, his brother may get mad over some trivial matter and then refuse to continue working. Consequently, he deliberately holds up the project, enrages his twin, and exercises passive-aggressive behavior. The parentified twin is often confused and mystified. Why is his twin treating him like this when all he tries to do is make his twin happy?

The parentified twin worries excessively if his twin is upset or sad. Usually, the parentified twin ends up giving in to the misbehaving twin because his ultimate goal is to avoid conflict. He is fearful about becoming more independent because he does not feel confident being on his own or relinquishing this role.

This dynamic borders on enmeshment, which evolves when two people have limited capacities to act as separate individuals. Being a separate person presupposes that one can tolerate disagreements, appreciate another's perspectives, and feel entitled to one's own feelings and needs. Helping young adult twins confront this troublesome conundrum is certainly possible; however, the longer twins remain in such an attachment pattern, the more difficult it is to disengage. A twin connection can be a complicated dyadic system.

The Caretaker Twin: She Needs You Too

A MOTHER OF THIRTEEN-YEAR-OLD fraternal twin girls asked my advice about how to help the cared-for twin develop more independent and self-confidence.

The mother remarked that both she and her husband give one twin special attention because she appears insecure and clingy. To their surprise, I suggested that they devote more time and attention to the caretaker twin because she may not be getting what she needs in terms of parental emotional investment.

Often, a child who is raised by "good enough" parents (parents who do the best they can, giving up the notion or expectation that perfection is possible when it comes to parenting) has her emotional needs satisfied and therefore usually grows up to be self-reliant and resilient. How can a twin who is busy taking care of her sibling be properly nurtured by a parental figure? This youngster may grow up feeling as if she has been emotionally neglected because her caretaking role has interfered with the fulfillment of her own longings.

Many parents of twins are unaware that the caretaker twin may grow up feeling as if her only function is to take care of others. As a result, she may miss out on the experience of being cared for, which can result in feelings of depression, emptiness, or existential angst. She cannot recognize her own needs because they were not sufficiently addressed, and she does not feel a connection to her unique self except when she is caring for another.

While this twin caretaking behavior appears loving and altruistic when twins are younger, too much interdependence may ultimately result in uncomfortable roles as they get older. One, or both, of the twins might want to free herself from this burdensome bond. However, either one may run the risk of upsetting the other by demanding change. Our role is to help our twins revere and respect their twin attachment rather than have it evolve into a strangulating connection that interferes with their development of uniqueness and individuality.

Do I Take Care of Myself or My Twin?

I RECEIVED AN EMAIL from Molly, a college-age female twin, who reached out to me because she was feeling worried and frustrated about her relationship with her sister Maddy. Although Molly and Maddy were now in their second year of attending separate colleges, Molly felt ongoing concerns about their twin relationship. Molly and Maddy are the eldest children, with three younger siblings. Molly described that she and her sister were basically treated as a unit most of their lives and that their family was consistently in the habit of glorifying the twin connection. When Molly was younger, she told her mom that she hated being a twin sometimes. Her mother became quite upset with her and reprimanded her not to say such things ever again.

Molly described herself as the caretaking twin in her relationship with Maddy. Even though they have been apart for some time now, Molly still feels responsible for Maddy's emotional well-being. When they are together, Molly feels compelled to try to help Maddy get out of a bad mood by emotionally suggesting that they do this or that. Also, if Maddy calls and is upset or needy, Molly reluctantly feels an obligation to listen and try to help her feel better. They have a much harder time being together now because they have lived on their own. Circumstances that used to be acceptable are difficult; for example, Molly likes things to be neat, and she cannot stand being around Maddy's messy room.

Molly asked me what I tell parents when they mention that their twins are not getting along. I teach parents that this discord is an expression of their twins' need to spend some time away from one another; it should be celebrated and valued because twins need to breathe on their own. Otherwise, how will they be able to grow up and be independent?

Soul Mates or Cell Mates?

HEALTHY ADULT TWINS do not feel imprisoned by their twinship. They have acknowledged each other's right to be separate and unique while maintaining their special connection. They have worked through feelings of ambivalence, competition, and jealousy, and each has evolved into an individuated self. Healthy twins care deeply about one another and recognize and respect each other's autonomy and choices. They enjoy being together but do not require exclusive possession of the other to cope with life or other relationships.

Some of my adult twin consultations focus on the difficulties that a number of adult twins encounter when one of the twins is moving in a developmental direction to be on her own while the other one is not. It is helpful to think about these troublesome adult twin transitions as codependent issues. Since numerous twin pairs have been emotionally reliant on one another for many years, they unwittingly develop an unhealthy dependence on one another. Very few people question this codependency because twins are expected to experience an extraordinary closeness.

In my book entitled *The Same but Different*, I address this issue of divergent twin agendas. For example, if one twin sister seeks a relationship outside of the twinship, both twins may experience difficulty coping with the new attachment. The twin in the new relationship feels guilty and selfish for "replacing" her sister, and the "abandoned" twin feels angry, resentful, and disappointed that she is no longer the first priority in her sister's life. These circumstances contribute to tremendous conflict, misunderstandings, and anguish for all concerned. The fact that so many twins and their families are not aware of these dynamics makes these inevitable consequences even more daunting.

Certain tips and suggestions may help to ameliorate the emotional tensions that bubble up when codependent behavior patterns are disrupted. First, one has to recognize and admit that one is an enabler. Enablers help people who are capable of doing things on their own. Enablers are the antithesis of helpers, who help empower people to do what they cannot do on their own. For example, twins often feel obligated to include their twin in their dating life because their sister is alone, jealous, and depressed. The content twin is emotionally conflicted about how to manage the connection and the separateness. How do twins nurture their new relationship and simultaneously sustain their loyalty and availability to their twin?

It requires tremendous patience and perseverance to tolerate painful or anxiety-provoking situations with one's twin that cannot be fixed. Twins have to be especially vigilant about not taking responsibility for their sibling's actions and about not being seduced back into the old relationship by feelings of guilt or selfishness. They must be consistent with newly drawn boundaries in terms of personal time and responsibilities.

Twins should reframe their mindset to reflect the feeling that they want to be around their twin rather than they need their twin around. There is an essential difference between missing one's twin and needing her. Twins must recognize that both need to develop new behaviors so that they can maintain their bond and nurture respectful attitudes about any new attachments in their lives. The process is similar to the progressive changes that children need to acclimate to following a separation, divorce, or second marriage. It requires time and acceptance, and it opens up the possibilities for newly created, healthy lifelong twin intimacy.

It's My Turn

A STUNNINGLY INTRANSIGENT aspect of the caretaker and cared-for twin dynamic is the fixed roles reflected in the dyadic interactions. The caretaker's sense of self-worth rests upon her success at lifting up her twin.

An identical twin in her midforties contacted me because she was worn out, depleted, and depressed after years of caring for her twin, who was diagnosed with bipolar disorder more than twenty years ago. She shared that her sister had been sickly since childhood and that her family made it her responsibility to look after her sister.

This woman consulted many therapists before getting in touch with me. She explained that each of them advised her to discontinue her caretaking role. Of course, this advice made practical sense; however, without understanding more about twin psychology, this suggestion had little impact other than to add to the patient's frustration and anger. A psychotherapist who understands the twin dynamic has to gently lay the groundwork for discovering the historical and developmental underpinnings of the client's emotional past.

This patient and I have worked together for several months. Her progress is extraordinary. She is confronting and working through the paralysis, shame, and resentment built up over years of feeling obligated to care for her sister. She intuits that her sister would not treat her as unselfishly if the tables were turned and my patient were ill. She acknowledges how much she allowed her personal growth and goals to be neglected in favor of her sister's psychological needs.

We have examined how my patient unknowingly sabotaged several educational and professional opportunities by feeling that she had to remain on call should her twin require immediate care. She never felt entitled to pursue her own dreams because her number one priority had to be lifting up her twin.

Similarly to many twins I have worked with, this woman has to come to terms with her role in this dyadic dance. She realizes that she avoided acting in her own interest over the years by rationalizing that this would interfere with her caretaking duties. On a deeper level, she complied with this pact because it offered protection from confronting her feelings of humiliation, social anxiety, and failure.

My patient is beginning to develop a sense of healthy entitlement. She has given herself permission to pursue an educational goal that heretofore seemed untenable. She has worked through some of the guilt over outshining her sister. She is attempting to reconcile being available to her sister and meeting some of her own needs. She is rediscovering her social skills and learning what it feels like to rely on herself. She has stopped introducing herself as a twin—a lifelong habit.

A few weeks ago, she shared an amazing experience. She participated in an outdoor team-building activity as part of her graduate program. She volunteered to be physically lifted up by her classmates in a trust-building exercise. As they cheered her on, she told me that she had never felt such a sensation of support and importance. I told her that it is her turn to be celebrated and recognized. I am confident that she will accomplish just that.

When Your Twin Becomes Your Child

INAUSPICIOUS CIRCUMSTANCES frequently arise when twins chronically adopt the roles of cared-for twin and caretaker twin. In many cases, this dynamic can evolve without any conscious awareness. It appears to originate organically from each twin's personality and role in the family. Some people believe that this paradigm begins in utero and increases exponentially as the twins mature. The pattern of one twin assuming a parental role toward his sibling is more likely to occur if one of the pair suffers more challenges and adversity than the other. The more fortunate twin instinctively adopts a protective and rescuing role; the wish to save his sibling—and more importantly, to feel needed—is an inherent function of the dynamic. The parenting twin unconsciously infantilizes his sibling. This interaction perpetuates a long-term dependency that can ultimately result in rancor and resentment. The longer this goes on, and the more adverse situations that the cared-for twin needs rescuing from, the more the caretaker sibling's parenting role becomes solidified and stagnant. The cared-for twin may resent his brother for being controlling and unreasonable. Their relationship becomes reminiscent of a parent and a child locked in a stifling conflict where neither will cede his ground.

Unfortunately, the caretaker twin often believes that his brother consciously recognizes the many sacrifices he has made and the countless times he has come to the rescue. However, when the tables are turned and the parentified twin needs support, his sibling often proves to be unavailable and unreliable. In light of the time, effort, and attention he devoted to his twin for so long, the rescuing brother is incredulous, enraged, and appalled at this self-centeredness and ingratitude.

The caretaker twin is horrified by his brother's cavalier attitude. He thinks, "How can my twin discount the innumerable times I helped him—for example, rescuing him from a terrible marriage, nurturing him through a contentious divorce, and being available to care for his children and pets on demand?" The parentified twin expects to be thanked, appreciated, and recognized in some fashion, but few of these expectations are realized. Meanwhile, the cared-for brother feels annoyed by his twin's needs and demands.

What is the final straw in these circumstances? Often, the breaking point happens when the parentified sibling realizes that the cared-for twin is happier and less needy. The caretaker twin feels enraged and betrayed because the only repayment he receives for his many sacrifices seems to be abandonment, lack of appreciation, and loneliness.

For twins in this situation, the lifelong roles of rescuer and rescued have constrained their perspectives and feelings. Unless they can come together as a couple and listen to each other's grievances and experiences, little can be done to save their twinship.

I Need to Be Needed and I Resent My Twin's Dependence

WHAT A DIFFICULT DILEMMA it is to grow up with your twin in a childhood caretaking role that may result in emotional turmoil as you mature. Unfortunately, and yet predictably, a divergence occurs frequently as twins approach adolescence and young adulthood. It stands to reason because at this developmental juncture, outside relationships with friends and romantic partners become salient and singular. Ironically, the caretaking twin may find this conundrum more conflictual because she has put many of her own needs and desires on the back burner. Suddenly she finds herself replaced, feeling resentful and burdened by the responsibilities she has either knowingly or unknowingly assumed. Twins who find themselves in these circumstances need wise parents or a qualified therapist to help them untangle some of the confusion.

Oftentimes parents are puzzled by what appears to be a horrific rift in their twins' connection. They are upset and worried that something is terribly amiss. They do not understand why or how such a lifelong close and loving attachment can be so quickly severed by a shift in the twin dynamics. Once parents can appreciate that twins need some separateness and space, they can relax and support them in their own respective emotional journey. Twins yearn for their parents to understand these longings without becoming distraught or offended. Otherwise, twins carry tremendous guilt about wanting to be "selfish," searching for independence and decisiveness.

Many older adult twins who have not managed to work through these struggles remain imprisoned in conflict, sadness, and hostility. Their twinship remains mired in older behavioral expectations and patterns that did not have the opportunity to be reworked to each twin's satisfaction or approval. Their inability to recognize and accept their differences becomes a barrier to their connection, sometimes giving rise to irreconcilable circumstances.

Twins: Self-Reliant or Selfish?

MANY TWINS WHO reach out to me for guidance struggle with anxiety about not feeling self-reliant. They realize that this conundrum relates significantly to growing up with a twin whom they relied on to feel secure, soothed, loved, and protected. Most have an intellectual understanding about these circumstances. They realize that their twin attachment constitutes their primary emotional security throughout their lives. Yet if one twin decides to form relationships outside the twinship and no longer feels invested in his twin role, his twin feels abandoned and lost. He is puzzled and confused about how to be independent after having spent so many of his precious early years depending on his twin to help navigate emotional hurdles.

Of course, this situation can present challenges for both siblings. While one twin seeks other intimate relationships, the abandoned twin continues to expect unfettered access to his twin's lifeline. He feels unequipped to be independent. How will he be able to be happy and resilient on his own?

How does a twin begin trying to define himself and find his place in the world as a nontwin? A helpful way to think about this struggle is to imagine how a singleton copes when he leaves home to attend a university where he knows no one. He has to muster social skills and self-confidence to meet many new people in an unfamiliar environment. It is an exceedingly challenging task for most young adults—even those who may have enjoyed previous social success.

A twin who has depended on his twin understandably finds this situation untenable and intolerable. He has not developed his own center of strength and stamina. One young woman described feeling as if she is on shaky ground or walking on uneven surfaces when she does not have her sister around to make her feel grounded and whole. This recognition of her neediness and dependency contributes to her feelings of abandonment, loneliness, and self-loathing. She is upset with herself about not being self-reliant, contributing to feelings of worthlessness, weakness, and vulnerability.

Twins need help branching out from each other in strategically healthy ways. Having the expectation that they can be friends rather than soul mates will hopefully set the stage for healthier future outcomes for twins and their families.

Part IV

YOUNG ADULT TWINS

How can a twin learn to embody and honor her authentic self when she has been raised to believe that her most valuable asset is her twin identity? It is no easy feat to discover one's uniqueness after spending a lifetime within a twin matrix.

Sometimes fights and arguments between twins signal the need—and the desire—to establish one's individuality. A young woman in her twenties recounts in this section that when her twin sister lashed out at her for no reason, it suddenly dawned on her that she was not at all responsible for her sibling's bad mood. In that moment, she was able to separate herself from whatever her sister was going through. Having worked hard in her therapy to feel distinct and differentiated from her sister, the altercation made her instantly aware of her singularity.

Since twins are accustomed to maintaining harmony and peace, overaccommodation is an adaptive tool. But overaccommodation requires that one is not true to one's feelings. In fact, in some instances, one may not even have access to their feelings because the only emotions that matter are those of the other person. A lifelong habit of being subjugated in this manner can lead to a person having limited ability to recognize their individuality. In other words, when one twin has grown up believing that emotional equilibrium is best managed by ceding control to the other, the compromising twin is unable to connect with his inner self.

What you'll hear about in this section is that it is indeed a struggle to feel like a separate person after years of feeling primarily like a twin. Individuating and owning one's authentic self involves motivation and insight. The shift in one's behavior and relationship to one's twin requires a transition to becoming what I call *selfish*. It means becoming aware of and celebrating your own needs, feelings, and thoughts without unduly worrying about your twin's position. When one has grown up identifying as half of a duo, it is indeed challenging to begin to identify as a singular person—thinking for oneself and trusting oneself without feeling guilt or shame.

Twins and Triangulation

IN MY WORK WITH adult twins, I often notice a tendency to manage conflict by engaging a third party. For example, an adult man channels his contempt for his brother by communicating this feeling to his twin's wife. He seems not to understand that this puts his sister-in-law in a bind. Should she be loyal to her husband or to her brother-in-law? Another young identical twin man introduces a female friend to his brother. Unbeknownst to him, the brother develops romantic feelings for this woman. As a result, both brothers are triangulated in their relationship with this young woman, with catastrophic repercussions for all. Or in another example, a female identical twin in her twenties who is estranged from her sister constantly talks to another family member about their conflicts and seems to deliberately air dirty laundry to implicate her sibling.

Triangulation can occur in any relationship pair, including family members, friends, romantic couples, and coworkers. It occurs frequently in twins since they are a well-honed dyad. This dynamic recruits a third person into the relationship so one member of the pair can remain in control. The triangulator controls communication between the two triangulatees. While triangulation may appear in different forms, the desired outcome is to divide and conquer.

Over time, triangulation alienates the twins even further as their conflicts spill over into other intimate relationships. What appears as sharing confidences with a third party is essentially tattling on the other sibling. Basically, one tries to justify one's feelings by persuading an outsider to take one's side. If you find that your relationship with your twin is heading in a precarious direction, find a therapist who can help you confront your issues together. Sometimes, all each sibling needs is to be heard within a safe space. While not every difficulty can be resolved, counseling can create an avenue for more direct cooperation and authentic communication in relationships.

Me First: Emotional Entitlement in Twinship

IF YOUR TWIN HAS BEEN the sole person meeting your emotional needs for most of your life, it can be challenging to recognize how nontwins might respond differently. Inseparable twin pairs develop an unarticulated rhythm that enables them to intuit what the other is thinking and react accordingly. For instance, if one twin is trying to get the other to change his plans to be with his brother, the twin needs little convincing to do so. Both are programmed to be alert to and cognizant of each other's needs so that a compromise is negotiated without argument or conflict. In many instances this fluid interaction is not even conscious until outside forces abruptly bring it into awareness.

An identical female twin in her midtwenties contacted me because she was beginning to feel uneasy and resentful toward her sister. She felt annoyed and intruded upon by her sister's incessant insistence that she drop whatever she was doing to be with her. Her twin repeatedly told her that she should join her to go shopping, swimming, or out to dinner. My patient resented these relentless demands to be together because she wanted to do things with other friends.

She felt torn between needing to appease her sister and wanting to be left alone. Predictably, she told me that she felt selfish about putting her own needs first, guilty about disappointing her sister, and angry that she felt so mired in this conundrum. She wanted to avoid conflict with her twin, as that had been a lifelong ingredient of their emotional connection. Moreover, she had difficulty handling her sister's anger and displeasure. She told me it was impossible to argue with her or give her advice because often they feel like one person.

We discussed how she could begin to take baby steps to establish some boundaries. While the process is extremely scary and difficult at the beginning, I stressed that changing her behavior might have a complementary effect on her sister. I explained that the emotional collusion that goes on between individuals who are overreliant on each other can evolve when one no longer colludes with the other. I gave the example that if one lives with an alcoholic and never says anything about the other's drinking, one plays an enabling role that perpetuates the problem.

I have noticed in my work with some of my twin patients that feeling entitled to their twin's unfettered emotional support leads to complicated situations in their other intimate relationships. Nontwins seek out emotional intimacy, of course. However, they may feel more inclined to work toward maintaining it rather than accepting that it is a ready-made, built-in feature of the connection.

Pretty in Pink

Two lovely twenty-two-year-old identical twin girls, Julie and Gemma, found me via my website. They are seniors in college, both pursuing the same degree. Julie told me that she and her sister have been fighting constantly. They are both unhappy living with each other. They have lived together for most of their college years. Both began freshmen year living with different roommates; however, by the second semester of their sophomore year, the girls moved in together because the twins' respective roommates wanted to live together. Julie explained that she and her sister dressed alike until they were ten years old. She told me that she was the twin who always dressed in pink. Her sister Gemma wore whatever other color clothing they were given. When they began college, Gemma finally had her turn to "own" the color pink. She did so by buying pink curtains for her room!

This story is complicated by another dynamic that has impacted their struggles to understand why they are having so many difficulties getting along. Throughout their lives, their mother has insisted on absolute togetherness and fairness. She becomes worried if one of them goes to the store without the other. The girls were looking forward to separate summer internships in different cities. However, their mother's anxiety and disapproval of the separation have negatively impacted the girls' excitement about this new chapter in their lives.

Both girls are aware that their fights have everything to do with their own desires and fears about separating from each other. If one decides to go shopping by herself and cook her own meals, the other twin will bake a dessert and refuse to share it with her sister because she is angry that her sister excluded her from her meals. We talked about these feelings being a metaphor for the struggles over separation that they are experiencing. Both teeter between wanting to separate, being angry that the other is excluding her by separating, and yet feeling guilty that one is excluding the other.

Although they have tried to differentiate themselves, many people cannot tell them apart. Teachers are always asking them who has better grades and even giving each one papers that belong to her sister. Both are at the top of their class scholastically. Neither has had another intimate relationship. They have seen a few different therapists who have not been able to help them understand the genesis of their fighting and annoyance with each other. Both are a bit frightened to be on their own but excited to confront the challenge.

Gemma told me that she was so angry with her sister during the Christmas holidays that she bought a copy of my book *The Same but Different* to give to her; Julie presented her sister with a sweatshirt that said "Twins Forever."

Hopefully they will be friends forever and will be able to work through the resentment and animosity they feel toward one another at this moment. Indeed, being compared and indoctrinated with the notion that everything between twins must be fair, these young women have issues to work through to discover and enjoy their individuality and uniqueness.

Separating Together

Often, twins who recognize they need a therapist's help to navigate treacherous emotional terrain can present with an extensive list of grievances about hostile, destructive, and mean behaviors. Usually, one twin in particular acts out by stealing away a best friend or romantic partner, sabotaging the completion of school or work projects, or refusing to share supplies or physical space.

However, my conjoint treatment of a pair of twenty-one-year-old identical twins, Casey and Francine, reveals no conscious anger; to the contrary, they are committed to helping each other separate and individuate. Both young women desperately desire to escape from their enmeshment. They are frightened by their lagging social and emotional development, which has been stymied by their unhealthy connection. While they love one another deeply, they astutely realize that their lives must change. They recognize that they need professional intervention and guidance to escape from a twin vortex that renders them fearful and paralyzed.

The girls describe an endless, compulsive cycle of misery and anxiety that began in high school and lasted through their college years. They had no awareness about their inability to self-regulate; they could only mutually regulate one another.

One recurring scenario in their dynamic played out as follows: Casey finished writing a paper. She saw that Francine was struggling and becoming increasingly frustrated. Francine began to cry. Casey could not feel accomplished or pleased with the job she did because she was overwhelmingly anxious about Francine's paralysis and fears. Casey dropped everything to come to Francine's rescue. Casey ended up writing the paper for Francine because she was inconsolable and distraught.

At the end of these episodes, neither twin was satisfied. Both described the experience as a shared frenzy that left them feeling empty, alone, and desperate. They were unable to enjoy their identical course of study because they were always in the same classes and working on shared projects. Both hated attending their university because all they did was study. Casey and Francine did acknowledge in retrospect that they hid behind a drive for academic success to rationalize avoiding social situations where they felt inept, out of place, and immature. They were too anxious to do activities with anyone else because their obsession with schoolwork left them no leisure time. They did not make friends or attend any social events. They shared a room and ate meals by themselves.

As I continue to work with them and they slowly individuate, I doubt Francine and Casey will develop that hostile, competitive edge that many twin pairs experience before realizing how much they long for separate identities. Both are optimistic that I will help them navigate their own individual paths. They seem to feel an almost parental love for one another. Consequently, one will make conscious sacrifices and compromises for the well-being of the other. While taking the highroad for the welfare of the other is a noble act, they will eventually need to address their individual expressions of ambivalence and disappointment as they move away from one another emotionally and confront the inequities they formerly avoided.

The Scrooge of Twindom

MY PRESENTATION AT the Budapest conference for the International Twin Society for Twin Studies and the World Congress of Twin Pregnancies conveyed my habitual passionate views about what twins require to become healthy individuals. I talked a bit about how parents struggle to differentiate and bond with two babies. Despite our best efforts, we default to labeling rather than describing each child. I am as guilty as the next person of labeling as it provides a shorthand communication that is quicker and more efficient. I also talked about how innocent remarks about each fetus made during ultrasound examinations can lead to assigning personality attributes after the babies are born.

I asked why the same parenting issues that have confronted families of twins for the last fifty years are still ever present. Even though there have been tremendous changes in terms of naming twins and dressing them differently, efforts to help them become individuals remain stultified. The advice from years past is still the same: help others distinguish between them, treat them as individuals, encourage them to do some things differently and some the same, encourage them to do what they need to do to separate from each other, and teach them to relate to others individually.

I suppose that our cultural obsession with twins has increased exponentially with the advent of the internet. News about twins that goes viral heightens the need to idealize the twin connection. Are the color-coordinated twins that were born holding hands destined to be best friends forever? Will they be given any opportunity not to become another twin stereotype? While at times I may appear to be the Scrooge of Twindom, I am a lonely voice crusading for twins' choices and lifestyles. I do not regard the challenges twins face as abnormal; rather, I am taking the challenges out from under the shadows of twin mysticism and helping twins embrace selfhood.

Best Friends . . . Bah, Humbug!

News about the healthy birth of monoamniotic (sharing the same amniotic sac) twin girls in Ohio went viral for a number of reasons. First, per a Cleveland.com article by the Associated Press, these births are rare (one in every ten thousand births) and often pose significant health risks to the unborn twins. The fetuses share a placenta and an amniotic sac but have separate umbilical cords. If unmonitored, strangulation might happen.

Naturally everyone was relieved and pleased about the positive outcome. However, most people seemed to be most captivated by the fact that the girls were born holding hands. The twins' mother gushed that the babies are already best friends. One reporter wrote that she was pretty sure that this hand-holding means these girls will never fight over their toys.

If I am the only person who feels upset and annoyed about this "best friend" expectation, I will explain why. As an identical twin, I have lived with this societal requisite to be my sister's best friend. If by some inexplicable lunacy this soul mate connection is not part of your twin experience, people somehow summarily dismiss you as an outcast in the twin cosmos. When my twin sister Jane and I tell people that we are sisters, that we love each other, and that we both have our own best friends, they seem disappointed and lose interest in continuing to talk about twins. While many twins are best friends and remain so throughout their lifetimes, many are not. It does not seem fair to stigmatize those who do not fit the stereotype.

I happen to believe that many twin pairs nurture their connection by putting some physical distance between themselves. They can maintain an emotional closeness that is modulated by some separateness. It is a bond that holds true to the adage, "Absence makes the heart grow fonder."

Constantly in Search of Acceptance

IT STANDS TO REASON that many of us who enter the helping professions have a fundamental proclivity for being helpful, and we enjoy feeling needed and appreciated. In the case of psychotherapists, our professional training, our ongoing personal therapy, and our continuing education enable us to secure and maintain healthy boundaries with our patients. While we experience tremendous gratification and a sense of well-being when our clients are doing well, we are careful not to consciously or unconsciously demand that our patients please us to satisfy our need to feel successful and relevant.

This constant search for acceptance is precisely what individuals in a codependent or enmeshed relationship crave. Certainly, one does not have to be a twin to find oneself in this unhealthy attachment. However, by virtue of their birth and upbringing, twins are paired with their same-age sibling throughout their lives. In many twin relationships, one twin takes on a caretaking role as a means of balancing personality dynamics. Consequently, such circumstances might put twins at risk for creating a codependent connection outside their will or control.

Codependency does not refer to all caring feelings or behaviors—only those that are excessive to an unhealthy degree. It often involves placing a lower priority on their own needs while being preoccupied with the needs of others. In doing so they forget to take care of themselves. Often codependent individuals cannot stand the thought of being alone and no one needing them. Feeling needed fuels the illusion of being in control of themselves and the other person. When the relationship is threatened by internal or external circumstances, both parties can experience tremendous anger, anxiety, and fear.

A young adult male twin in his late twenties whom I work with has tremendous difficulty figuring out his identity, passion, and direction. He has grown up being concerned about the well-being of his twin brother. He did not give much thought to his own needs or feelings; his role was to enhance and ensure his brother's safety and sense of self. My patient had no conscious idea what he was doing or why. He was content to believe that he held the key to his brother's happiness and welfare. He had no reason to question or doubt his caretaking role until his brother began dating a girl in their sophomore year of college. When his brother's loyalties shifted to this new intimate other, my patient's emotional world fell apart. His identity and self-definition collapsed instantaneously like a house of cards. If he was no longer his brother's best friend and core caretaker, who was he?

Eventually he will be able to discover what he wants; however, he has to work through years of not knowing himself or even thinking about himself. What he imagined would always be his everlasting source of self-esteem and security has to be mourned to make psychological room for an emerging sense of who he is and who he will become.

Butt Out!

I FREQUENTLY HEAR from moms looking for help with their adult twins. In most instances, the issues involve one sibling doing better than the other. The mom feels particularly conflicted when one twin is thriving while the other is struggling. Her desire to equalize the situation is understandable. However, her intervention may actually polarize the state of affairs even further. The mom's well-intentioned efforts to help her discontented daughter may result in both girls feeling unhappy and undermined. While this same dynamic might happen among different-age siblings, twins feel particularly vulnerable because they have been compared and competitive for most of their lives.

Feeling powerless to fix the problems, the mom will often attempt to coerce the flourishing twin to help solve her sibling's issues. Tara, a twin in her late twenties, found herself in these exact circumstances. Her identical twin, Terrie, has a history of physical and emotional problems that Tara has helped to manage since their sophomore year of college. Since then, Terrie has been plagued with several somatic and emotional complaints that appear endless and untreatable. The twins' mother has tried her utmost best to provide medical and psychiatric treatments to address these various issues; however, none of them have worked for Terrie. She still experiences tremendous pain and serious depression. Even though she is married and able to work, she remains angry with her parents and her sister for not making her life better.

Terrie constantly berates Tara for accomplishing goals Terrie has been unable to attain. For instance, Tara plans to attend graduate school, which angers Terrie because she could not finish her undergraduate studies due to her own chronic physical problems. She has little empathy for others and seems incapable of taking responsibility for her own behavior. She inevitably initiates confrontations with Tara about inconsequential past events because that gives Terrie a sense of control.

Tara misses the healthy Terrie. She tears up when recalling their intimate moments and shared confidences. Nonetheless, Tara is happier now because she has worked diligently to become separate from her sister without feeling intolerable guilt. She no longer wants to be burdened by or held responsible for her twin's struggles. Moreover, her relationship with her mom has become more honest and authentic. In a conjoint session, Tara was able to tell her mom how upset she feels when her mom deliberately downplays Tara's successes in Terrie's presence so she does not feel devalued. The mom quickly understood Tara's perspective and apologized for her inability to manage the discrepancies between the twins. Tara also said that she thought her mom enabled Terrie to get away with insufferable behavior because the mom felt guilty and sad about Terrie's plight. Tara's mom agreed and has been working on minimizing those tendencies.

I constantly reiterate that life is not fair, and twins are not equal. The earlier parents become comfortable with inequities, the sooner their twins can embrace their individuality and feel freer to be themselves in the face of inevitable differences.

Can She Be Happy for Me?

MANY TWIN PAIRS successfully juggle jealous feelings, recognizing their disparities and living comfortably with their ambivalence. For example, "I am jealous of your financial success, *and* I am happy you don't have worries about money." Or "I am jealous that your children are married, *and* I wish them nothing but happiness." Or "I am jealous that you are getting married before me, *and* I am so pleased you have found love and happiness."

Authentic acknowledgment of these ambivalent feelings is vital to keeping love intact in the face of anger and resentment evoked by competition and comparison. Twins who achieve this level of individuation are in touch with their separate selves. Hence, they are capable of self-reflection while also listening to and recognizing the perceptions and feelings of another. They take responsibility for their thoughts and triggers while simultaneously managing upsetting responses from their twin.

An identical twin woman in her thirties related an interesting anecdote that highlights this dynamic. She and her sister have always been quite competitive with each other. In their individual therapy sessions, each has worked hard to understand her twinship issues. As a result, both have become more tolerant and forgiving of the other. While they have frequent misunderstandings and conflicts, these misattunements no longer lead to ruptures or devastating consequences.

My patient has worked diligently to separate emotionally from her sister. She had always felt like the inferior, defective twin who would do anything to win her twin's approval and love. She grew up craving her sister's attention and inclusion. Her sister's demand that she be the life of the party led her to behave in ways that did not reflect her authentic self. Desperate to make her sister happy, she was ready, willing, and able to enact her sister's requisites. At times this included gaining weight, getting drunk, or enduring hostile barbs. When a long-term rupture did occur, she felt lost, alone, abandoned, and bereft.

Now she can feel good about herself without her sister's endorsement. Nevertheless, if she feels that her sister cannot or will not be happy for her, she is disappointed. Although she no longer needs mirroring from her sister to sustain her self-esteem, she longs for the closeness and connection that they once shared. She has learned to manage the frustration and not turn it into a combative bout. This action requires a high level of emotional intelligence not easily achieved without therapeutic intervention.

Just as singleton children and adults yearn for parental love and approval, twins who grow up without this vital developmental ingredient end up providing it to each other. While this proves to be a source of comfort for twins at that moment, this dynamic can become infused with ugly competitiveness as the twins mature and often becomes a complicated process to dissect and digest.

Needing a Best Friend

SARAH, A YOUNG ADULT female identical twin, struggles with her female friendships. Although she has many close friendships, her longing to be the "one and only" best friend consumes her. While she has an intellectual understanding about this issue being inextricably linked to her twinship, emotionally she gets stymied. She is constantly bothered, upset, and perhaps a bit obsessed by her friends' other intimate connections. The idea that she cannot be number one makes her feel devalued, unimportant, and unloved.

Sarah's constant tension about needing a best friend is linked to being her twin's devotee and best friend. Her sister was extroverted, confident, and focused. Sarah remained behind the scenes so as not to eclipse her sister in any way. She believed that there would be an enormous payback for such sacrifices—being her twin's best friend forever. However, her sister's intimate connection with another shattered these expectations.

Sarah has worked diligently in treatment to attempt to come into her own—feeling that she is a desirable person who deserves people in her life who can admire her and cherish her. She can identify and articulate these feelings in the context of her twin connection. She can share some of these misgivings with her good friends so that her needy behaviors can be put into another perspective. She must consistently reframe her negative feelings so she can stay positively regulated in her interactions.

Certainly we are aware of how societal, cultural, and familial expectations demand that twins be best friends. If they are not, parents and twins themselves feel as if they have let everyone down. Sarah realizes that her longing for a best friend is connected to replacing her twin attachment. More than likely, the replacement twin relationship reflects important qualities that mirror the twin connection.

Many twin pairs seek a soul mate to replicate the extraordinary closeness and unconditional love they experienced in their childhood. Twins who escape this indoctrination are truly blessed. They authentically can enjoy and love their twin without resentments and disappointments.

Part V

ROMANTIC AND MARITAL RELATIONSHIPS INVOLVING TWINS

SOME TWINS CANNOT make room in their life for a third person, especially for their twin's significant other. Twins who are threatened by their same-age sibling's romantic or marital partner perceive the twinship as a sealed space, sacred and fundamental, taking absolute precedence over any other relationship. When one twin connects with an intimate other and becomes more emotionally involved with that person than with their sibling, the nonattached twin can feel replaced, betrayed, enraged, and bereft. They cannot imagine life without the ongoing primacy of the twin connection, so when an outside connection is forged, they may feel as if their sacred bond has been broken. It's almost as if a twin having a romantic partner goes against nature itself because, in the eyes of the bereft twin, the love between twins is priority number one.

Although twins may intellectually understand the need for romantic involvement and marriage, they can still be incredulous when their sibling feels closer to a partner than to them and "leaves" them for that person. Replaced twins may even feel out of control and devastated, questioning how they will be able to carry on under such altered circumstances.

As the essays in this section show, the partner or spouse of a twin is often stunned and overwhelmed by the chaos and drama that ensues when two become three. The partner may have limited understanding about how such a normal developmental shift can create such upheaval.

Additionally, the partnered twin may become incensed, for example, that his brother is not happy for him. He insists that if the tables were turned, he would welcome the partner into the family and not treat his twin so shabbily. Or he may struggle with feelings of guilt, worried that his twin brother won't be able to handle the shift in the twinship, which leaves him unable to feel happy and entitled to his new relationship.

Must twins give up their close connection to enjoy a romantic relationship? Can partners of twins learn to accommodate—or at least understand—a sibling who competes for the love and attention of the partnered twin? Working through these relationship conflicts is achievable if same-age siblings and partners learn to make compromises.

Find Your Comfort Zone and Leave It

I WAS LISTENING TO an NPR piece called "Wisdom from YA Authors on Leaving Home: Neal Shusterman." The author Neal Shusterman reminisced about his troubled adolescence adjusting to life in a new country. He related that overcoming depression and loneliness was instrumental in the future adaptations he had to make throughout the course of his life. His advice was "find your comfort zone and then leave it."

This radio piece resonated with me professionally and personally. In my clinical work with patients, I try to help my clients work through their anxiety and fears about taking risks and tolerating failures. With my adult children I will always be the maternal source for support and security when life's inevitable challenges play out unfairly. When I give presentations to parents of twins, I always talk about the importance of creating resilience in twins by creating separate situations and experiences for the twins to manage without each other's support.

Assessing when a twin's comfort zone is too influenced by the attachment to the other twin can be difficult. A young woman in her thirties contacted me because she was upset about a lengthy, conflicted divorce that seemed to drain her emotional and physical strength. Her twin lived in a nearby state, so they were geographically able to get together without too much difficulty, and they talked to each other on a daily basis.

As we talked, it became clear that her marriage had been adversely affected by her connection to her sister. Her ex-husband resented her magnetic investment in her twin and attempted to thwart their connection whenever possible. The divorce has triggered her sadness and anxiety about being separated from her sister. Both grew up together in a small town and did everything together. Since their mother was estranged from the family, both women were put in the position of parenting one another. Understandably, this dependence on one another in the face of no maternal sustenance deepened their attachment to each other.

To work through some of the marital issues she did not want to repeat, she attempted to gain more insight into her relationship with her sister. Intellectually she recognized that her intense need for and connection to her sister got in the way of finding other nurturing attachments. She had struggled to find a therapist who can be empathic and sympathetic about her twin connection. She told me that no one seems to understand her issues and that people dismiss her concerns as crazy and weird.

Twins who have parented one another throughout their lives without adequate guidance and support will have expectable struggles finding and trusting others to rely on. Whenever we are required to leave our comfort zone, we need to know that we can fall gently and quietly. I picture myself falling back on a fluffy down comforter—burying myself in the soothing feathery splendor and then getting back on my feet to contemplate my next move.

Loving a Twin: An Emotional Roller Coaster

I RECEIVED AN EMAIL from a distraught young woman describing how her boyfriend of five years struggles with divided loyalties between her and his identical twin brother. The young woman says that her boyfriend's twin frequently requires rescuing due to chronic problems with drug use and unemployment. Her boyfriend's family has always been insistent that he take care of his less fortunate twin. The family resents their son being in a committed relationship because it derails his commitment to his brother's care. As a result, they blame the girlfriend for fragmenting the twin attachment.

I imagine that the young woman writing this email is at her wit's end. Either consciously or unconsciously, she must feel defeated and frustrated that her boyfriend seems unable to make significant decisions so that she can get on with her life—with or without him. She is certainly not being treated with the respect and devotion she deserves. I think she was initially optimistic that her boyfriend would find a solution to this conundrum. She had no idea when she became involved with this young man that his twinship might lead to a breakup.

However, as many intimate partners of twins discover, some twins suffer from tremendous heartache, sadness, and a sense of betrayal when they switch their allegiance away from their sibling. My heart goes out to all the involved parties. This disconcerted young man has been forewarned by his family that refusing to accommodate his twin's needs will result in being abandoned by the rest of his family members. So he must choose between his loving girlfriend and his demanding family.

Sadly, this scenario is not terribly uncommon. One gentleman shared his experience of being married to an identical twin. Fortunately for both him and his wife, they had a nine-year relationship before they married, and he helped his wife navigate many of the separation difficulties that arose between the sisters. Those long years together facilitated a smooth transition to new dyadic and triadic dynamics.

With a big smile on his face, this gentleman told me a story about the twin sisters. At his wedding, his wife's twin was the maid of honor; she defiantly wore tennis shoes rather than dress shoes underneath her gown. She claimed not to have had time to buy an appropriate pair of wedding shoes. Both he and his wife were able to laugh about her twin's passive-aggressive behavior rather than feel angry or disrespected.

When I give presentations, I often discuss the struggles of the many people who contacted me over the years about the emotional difficulties of being involved with a twin. Men and women alike have suffered because of their significant other's relationship with a twin sibling. I frequently muse that twins who marry twins skillfully avoid this emotional upheaval.

When a Wedding Feels Like a Funeral

Tom, a depressed and downtrodden thirty-five-year-old identical twin, told me that his brother's upcoming wedding will feel like a funeral rather than a wedding. Since his brother began dating his fiancée about two years ago, Tom has been withdrawn and emotionally shut down. He was unable to attend family functions that included his twin and the fiancée because he felt that he could not be present or authentic.

While this young man can intellectualize his feelings of abandonment, grief, and sadness, he has a limited ability to feel them. He dreads not showing up at his brother's wedding because his absence will devastate his family, his twin, and himself. He recognizes that he has been emotionally paralyzed for the last few years since his brother first introduced his girlfriend to the family.

Tom's family is upset about his inability or unwillingness to move forward. The family has candidly discussed the situation; however, for some reason, Tom seems to have little motivation to work through his depression. He either cannot or will not follow through with psychotherapy or entertain the notion of medication. While the twinship certainly plays a substantial role in Tom's issues with his brother, the broken twin connection also seems to have revealed other emotional factors previously well hidden behind the twin façade.

Judging by Tom's story, I surmise that the twinship formerly provided a defensive bulwark to ward off feelings and anxieties he does not want to confront. I intuit that many of these feelings involve unresolved fears about his social insecurities, which predate his brother's upcoming marriage.

This case highlights how the twin bond may stymie maturation, leaving the twins ill equipped to manage peer pressure, outside friendships, and societal expectations. While speculating about what might have occurred if Tom faced these issues as a singleton is moot, these circumstances do illustrate how a loving twin relationship can unconsciously derail expectable developmental behaviors for one or both twins.

Betrayal: Treacherous Twin Territory

THE NONTWIN PUBLIC may struggle to understand why a twin's experience of betrayal is more intense than what a singleton might ever imagine. For many twin pairs, the loss of one's twin to another relationship is profound. The twin loses more than just exclusive access. He forfeits the sense of security, safety, and love that he has come to depend on his whole life.

The twin connection is his assurance that all is right with the world and that he can count on the relationship to fulfill his social and emotional needs. He cannot afford to contemplate any outside threat to this arrangement because his integration and happiness rest on this ongoing arrangement.

A pair of nineteen-year-old identical twin men experienced such a disruption. Neither had much of a social life in high school. The twins, Roger and Reggie, tended to stick together out of habit and comfort. Both were looking forward to attending different colleges. However, similar to other young adults, the pandemic forced them to begin their studies virtually at home. Both enjoyed playing video games and did so online with others. Roger became friendly with a female gamer, Adele, and introduced her to Reggie. Unbeknownst to Roger, Reggie and Adele began to text one another frequently and developed a close relationship. Adele also stayed in touch with Roger but did not divulge her deeper connection to Reggie.

Eventually, Roger uncovered the deception and flew into a rage with his twin. It was at this point that their mother contacted me. Her sons had never fought openly about anything. She noted the pride she felt about having a wonderfully happy family. She could never understand why so many other parents complained about sibling rivalry. She explained that Roger was having the most difficulty. He was depressed, tearful, and shut down; he rejected offers of support from her as well as Reggie. In fact, he was not talking to his brother at all. This situation made life at home very unsettling, tense, and sad.

Thankfully, I was able to see Roger for several in-person sessions. Eagerly he assimilated the tenets of twin psychology to understand why he was so emotionally distraught. Throughout our work together, it came to light that Roger idealized Reggie. Roger was the dominant caretaker in their relationship, happily accommodating Reggie's wants and needs. He did so without rancor or protest. He honestly felt magnanimous about his willingness to compromise and take a backseat. However, when Reggie's deceptive affair with Adele surfaced, so did Roger's pent-up indignation. He related that Reggie's betrayal was unforgivable and that their bond was forever severed.

In our sessions together, the anger subsided and the sadness surfaced. Roger began to recognize the part that he had played in the twinship. He came to realize how he had compromised himself for the benefit of the twinship. The rift was, in truth, a gift that revealed how his relationship had impacted his identity, sense of self, and self-confidence. Our discussions about his envy of and competition with Reggie contributed to Roger's feeling of being undermined and ripped off. In one poignant joint session with Reggie, Roger explained many of his feelings and regrets. Reggie listened with patience and compassion.

While the rivalry concerning Adele did last for a couple more months, the twins' willingness to communicate their feelings about the circumstances facilitated a much-needed appreciation for separation and space from each other. Reggie left for a week to visit a relative. It was the first time the boys had ever been apart from each other. They came to realize that the betrayal was not just about Adele. It went much deeper than that. It engendered a treacherous breach in their twinship, compromising their idyllic relationship. Their individuality required definition and direction, and their relatedness needed recalibration.

Often, maturational growth follows a crisis. When expectations and affiliations are modified, an authentic harmony can emerge.

Honesty Is Only the First Step

As a seasoned clinician, I am well aware that insight is the gateway to change. I tell my patients that discovering fresh insights into our problems and ourselves is akin to opening a window that has previously been shuttered or stuck. However, to discover those insights, we must open that window to risk new behaviors and experiences that may feel out of reach or simply too intimating to contemplate.

I was communicating electronically with an adult twin woman in her late twenties about why her relationship with her sister is so stultifying. She chronicled how their competitive strivings made both of them feel exquisitely sensitive to comparison. Also, she was quick to point out how their birth circumstances defined their dyadic roles: her sister's lower birth weight contributed to her sister being treated as the baby and consequently catapulted her into the role of the caretaking twin.

This woman was in a serious romantic relationship, and her twin was not. Although she mentioned that she and her sister had talked openly about the possible ramifications of her getting married and moving away, it seemed clear that this woman's expectable fears and tremendous guilt about moving forward had been paralyzing. She had been putting off her own marriage and future with excuses related to work and living conditions.

I urged her to find a therapist nearby to help her move through the psychic turmoil that she'll have to confront to open the window to a new life—to physically and emotionally separate from her twin. I suggested that she confront these issues sooner rather than later. Otherwise, feelings of bitterness and despair will exponentially grow if she sacrifices her happiness to preserve the twin connection.

My Husband's Twin Brother Moved Next Door

I HAVE WRITTEN OFTEN about how partners of twins have difficulty understanding the depth and pull of twinship. Diane recently reached out for help to handle her feelings of resentment and helplessness about her husband's renewed and intensified relationship with his twin brother.

She explained that, in the past, she had a terrific relationship with her brother-in-law. However, since his contentious divorce and his move next door to her family, she has felt left out and abandoned. When she expresses her discontented feelings to her husband about this situation, he becomes angry and cannot figure out why her feelings about his twin brother have changed. Her husband tells her that he has to be very available to his twin because he is feeling vulnerable and lonely. In her view, her husband seems to have little empathy for the fact that she feels abandoned as well.

I asked her to tell me more about the twin brothers' upbringing. She explained that the boys essentially raised each other because their father left the home when they were young, and their mother was an alcoholic who worked to support the family. They parented one another, acting as each other's best friend, supporter, and parental surrogate.

I talked to Diane about their connection—how they held on to each other for emotional and physical survival. In the face of his brother's dilemma, Diane's husband feels obligated to take care of his brother to the exclusion of other intimate connections. I related that her husband must be feeling extraordinarily guilty because his brother is in emotional turmoil while he is not.

After Diane understood the circumstances from an empathic stance, she felt more confident about bringing up the subject with her husband. Her husband responded well to this approach, breaking down and confiding that he was feeling helpless and overwhelmed about not being able to help his brother feel better; moreover, he experienced tremendous guilt because he was not suffering. He explained that he and his brother worked hard to keep a balance between them when they were growing up because it felt unbearable for one to have more than the other. His brother's unstable circumstances have triggered his feelings of responsibility for his brother's well-being once again and caused discomfort about the inequality that exists between them at present.

Talking about this with his wife helped Diane's husband recognize that he could not "save" his brother, as he believed he could and should. He followed her advice and helped convince his brother to find a therapist to help him work through his issues. This arrangement helped to empower Diane and her husband so they could act as supportive allies, not rescuers.

Love Cannot Conquer All—Even Twin Love

As so many of us discover after a number of years of marriage, the exact qualities that attracted us to our beloved turn out to be personality traits that may contribute to our feeling unhappy, lonely, or sad later on in the relationship. This predicament can become especially intolerable if you have a twin who gets you, has your back, demonstrates unconditional love and acceptance, and needs to hear no more than a few words drop from your lips to instantaneously and empathically understand what you're going through.

The fortunate twin pairs who have this loving and inherent connection may feel disappointed and angry when their spouses don't and can't measure up to this unparalleled intimacy. These closely bonded twins may expect that this unbridled connection will or should automatically reoccur when they marry and have a family. However, it's important for all of us—not just twins—to think about what preceded our falling in love and how that impacted and influenced our choices of mates.

I had the pleasure of speaking with an identical twin woman in her forties who contacted me about her disappointment with her husband's lack of mirroring. In fact, she told me that both she and her twin sister often feel lonely in their marriages because they cannot get from their husbands what they organically share with one another. As I probed more into her history, she told me that both she and her sister had been competitive snow skiers. Their father had been a ski instructor, and at seven years of age both girls began to ski. With their dad as their coach, both women achieved extraordinary professional success and enjoyed celebratory careers.

As she talked a bit more, she had an aha moment, recognizing that both she and her sister married highly independent men. She reflected that their choice of mates had much to do with the fact that they had been under their father's control for so many years. For better or worse, their underlying need to please and perform for him unconsciously enhanced their attraction to men who appeared self-contained.

So now the self-sufficient guy whom she fell in love with in college cannot fulfill her wishes for emotional intimacy, as he has never been that kind of man. He is a loving husband and father whom she loves and admires; nonetheless, the persistent loneliness she feels must be addressed through her own willingness to find more intimate connections with girlfriends or colleagues. Accepting and understanding the limitations of her marital intimacy and recognizing the uniqueness of her twin intimacy, she is comfortable looking outside of these connections to find friendship and companionship.

Emotional Blackmail

As occurs frequently among twins, tensions escalated significantly between Jamie and her twin sister, Jackie, when Jamie began dating her first boyfriend at the age of nineteen. Jackie complained frequently that Jamie was spending too much time with her boyfriend.

Jamie was torn apart emotionally. She loves her sister and is heartbroken that Jackie becomes angry and nasty when Jamie is away with her boyfriend. Intellectually, Jamie knows that she is entitled to her romantic relationship; however, she is conflicted about Jackie's accusations that she is abandoning her and choosing this outsider over her.

The girls have always been very close. Jamie has taken on the caretaker role because she has been able to navigate her social and academic life with a bit more success than her sister. Jackie relies on her twin to be her sole confidant and rescuer, refusing to tell any other family members what she feels or is going through.

Jamie described what happens repeatedly when Jackie argues with her. Jackie will accuse Jamie of betraying her or letting her down. When Jamie attempts to share her side of the story or her recounting of the events, Jackie gets upset. In such moments Jamie becomes paralyzed. She tries to share her point of view but is frozen emotionally in the face of Jackie's anger. Thus, she shuts down and cannot articulate her feelings, needs, or free will.

This emotional freezing by one partner in a codependent relationship occurs frequently. Whether in a twinship or a marriage, if one party does not have the freedom to assert oneself or one's feelings, the partner exerts control and power and the other shuts down. This can evolve into a toxic situation that can result in emotional and physical abuse. Sadly, Jamie is controlled by Jackie's feelings and becomes incapable of asserting herself in their conflict-laden interactions.

Jamie's dawning awareness about her position in this twinship is daunting. She had no reason to think about such twin issues before her boyfriend came on the scene. She habitually accepted the role she played without question or fear. She has quite a long way to go to begin to get her head around the present situation. Yet better now than later as this dynamic can worsen with time and age. It is incredibly sad that her first romantic encounter has incurred her twin's wrath, making her feel guilty, undeserving, and unhappy.

Part VI

OLDER ADULT TWINS

WHILE NONTWIN SIBLINGS often compare themselves to a sister or brother in terms of skills and talents, accomplishments, and romantic relationships, for twins, comparison and competition can be ongoing. Some twins experience being compared and competitive their entire lives, especially if their parents haven't adequately encouraged them to perceive themselves as distinct individuals.

Too often, twins are saddled with labels that define them as the exact opposite of their same-age sibling—for example, "the quiet one" versus "the gregarious one" or "the artist" versus "the business guy." Unfortunately, our culture mythologizes twins and tends to support such neat categorization: "Mary behaves this way, and Melissa is the extreme opposite." Those who buy into this erroneous mindset find this system an easy way to differentiate siblings who were born on the same date. Breaking free from such limiting comparisons can be a developmental challenge for twins. Also challenging is learning to calibrate healthy competition with one's twin when skill sets are evenly matched and both siblings gravitate toward similar interests.

This section includes stories from older twins who continue to contend with a competitive dynamic that complicates their emotional well-being. For example, one twin feels the need to outdo her sister in becoming too thin, another considers herself unsuccessful if her career fails to take off like her sister's, and a single brother pushes himself into marriage to "keep up" with his married twin.

To alleviate unhealthy competition and comparison, same-age siblings can come to understand that both deserve their own pursuits, goals, and sense of self.

Adult Twins: Identity, Rivalry, and Intimacy

SOME TWIN PAIRS—though not all—become disillusioned about their twinship because they struggle to be "known," not just "noticed." Since outsiders habitually relate to them as a unit or a fixed dyad, they expectedly have conflicts with their twin in an attempt to define or declare their individual selves. While twins fight just like different-age siblings, their tensions have much more to do with establishing separateness and uniqueness, traits afforded naturally to siblings born at different times.

Twins, especially identical twins, appear to harbor more resentment toward one another as they get older because they have worked diligently to establish a balanced and harmonious relationship over the course of their lives. They have both invested in this balance out of a need and wish to regulate competition and comparison. As their lives diverge, it becomes much more difficult to maintain a sense of equality and sameness. When this occurs, one twin might find it difficult to enjoy her work or relationship successes because she feels guilty about disrupting the balance with her sister. I have worked with many twins who feel as if they are betraying and abandoning their twin when their life paths diverge and change. Their loyalties to one another are strong—while admirable, it makes separation much more difficult. Rivalry in adult twins has everything to do with wanting to be on one's own and discovering one's singular sense of self without worrying how this will disrupt and upset one's twin.

My work with twins has also highlighted why they have difficulty handling conflict. Rather than agreeing to disagree or being capable of hearing their twin's perspective, they are more driven to win rather than compromise. I believe this lack of emotional maturity results from the fact that they are still struggling to come to terms with their individual identities and therefore are still fighting to beat their rival rather than respectfully accept their differences. Isn't it ironic that twins who are perceived as soul mates and "best friends forever" often have difficulty with the most basic concepts of intimacy—compromise, empathy, and acceptance of differences?

The deep dependency issues that naturally evolve growing up as a twin also fuel twin rivalry. So often twins are behind their singleton peers in achieving developmental mastery.

They go to sleep, go to school, socialize, and study with their twin. While this togetherness has definitive benefits, it can also interfere with each twin's capacity to be resilient and independent. By the time twins go to college, they are expected to be capable of handling many life tasks as an individual. However, without any prior planning or preparation, they are understandably ill equipped to handle many situations on their own.

Most twin pairs eventually find ways to repair their relationships and mitigate their rivalry as they find and define their individual life paths and identities.

Not Seeing Eye to Eye: The Eye of the Twinship Storm

MANY OF THE ADULT TWINS that contact me are experiencing emotional pain due to a growing awareness that they are different from their twin. They struggle mightily with this dawning realization that they are not magically and nonverbally on the same page. Often, external circumstances trigger a series of events that make a twin pair's differences obvious. For example, becoming a parent for the first time can be a tumultuous developmental adjustment for many people. When one twin discovers that her sibling is critical of her maternal decisions, she may be surprised and disturbed to realize that she and her twin do not think alike. Unfortunately, disagreements between twins can devolve over time into a disheartening inability to accept what each other is saying or doing. Twins often feel utter disbelief that their twin could be so harsh, unsupportive, and opinionated.

Naturally, these feelings highlight an inability to handle differences that eventually results in a nasty, vicious contest to prove who is right and who is wrong. While it is not uncommon for siblings to have very different parenting styles, this does not have to lead to a disruption in their connection. In the best of circumstances, they can agree to disagree without causing a major communication breakdown.

However, for some twin pairs, disagreements are not an option. Their arguments do not play out as two separate persons asserting their views and thoughts; rather, dissenting opinions seamlessly morph into feelings of rejection and wrongdoing. In severe circumstances, such discord may result in twins deciding not to talk to one another.

The sad truth is that neither one of them truly understands why their relationship deteriorated. Most likely, their contrasting styles of relating or living highlighted significant disparities that were not dyadically managed throughout the twins' lives together. So their differences disrupt the progression of a seemingly harmonious lifetime bond. Unbeknownst to them, the twinship inhibited them from experiencing opportunities to process and manage expectable conflict.

Nonetheless, seeking professional intervention from a knowledgeable psychotherapist can offer some guidance about why their twin connection broke down. Hopefully, the twin pair will eventually understand that disagreements do not have to end in dissolution if both parties can be receptive to the other's state of mind and respect each other's personal subjectivity.

Envy: The Spoiler

ENVY IS A CONSEQUENCE of many human interactions. Envying something or someone can be a motivating influence to work toward getting what you'd like for yourself. Or, to the contrary, hateful envy can lead to damaged relationships and disastrous outcomes.

Many twin pairs have definitive tendencies toward envious behaviors. This is understandable in light of how much they are compared to each other and viewed as a dyadic couple rather than two separate individuals. Contemplating the many pairs of twins I have seen in my practice over the years, I am curious about the specific dynamics that have contributed to the development of envy rather than jealousy.

Jealousy is a common emotion—most of us can admit to ourselves or others when we wish we had what others had or resent those who have what we don't. Being able to admit to and articulate jealous feelings is important so that they are not accompanied by excessive feelings of guilt or shame.

Envy, on the other hand, is a more pernicious feeling in that the individual who envies another feels tremendous hostility, anger, and resentment. One who envies another may harbor threatening thoughts toward the envied person. This sinister continuum includes many degrees of viciousness; however, a common thread is that the individual who envies another may consciously or unconsciously wish or enact emotional or physical harm on the other.

The twins I have worked with who have had to contend with an extremely envious twin have a difficult path. Depending on the severity of the resentment, some twins have felt the need to become estranged from their envious twin if there appears to be no room for working out these feelings. In other situations, the twin who is envied recognizes that she is her sibling's moving target and takes precautions to protect herself when she can.

I am reminded of a pair of forty-year-old identical twin women who suffer with this envy dilemma. Tilly sought treatment with me because her sister's mean and humiliating treatment seemed unwarranted. Tilly was clueless as to why her twin, Tracy, was often rude and demeaning almost out of the blue. When she asked Tracy why she was acting this way, Tracy shrugged off Tilly's comments and feelings as absurd and exaggerated.

Tilly's history provided some explanation for the present circumstances. In addition to being their mother's favorite, Tilly was the outgoing, popular twin. She had been highly emotionally intelligent from a young age. As a result, she garnered attention and love from others that Tracy did not receive. Tilly earned a well-paid professional salary, had a loving husband and two small children, and demonstrated a happy and positive outlook on life in general.

Tracy also enjoyed her professional life, although she was not as highly salaried, and she was happily married with three children. Notwithstanding her own successes, Tracy never lost an opportunity to denigrate Tilly. She criticized Tilly's spouse and made spurious judgments about her children.

Tilly attempted to handle Tracy's mean comments and threats by telling herself that Tracy was jealous of her. Tilly felt guilty that her life was proceeding so well and that Tracy seemed to be struggling in ways that she was not. Tilly called me when she could no longer tolerate the negativity. Her coping skills were wearing thin, and she craved more understanding and insight.

Our work together focused on helping Tilly understand the nuances between jealousy and envy. Envy can feel vilifying and annihilating. Tilly had difficulty accepting that Tracy harbored such destructive tendencies toward her. However, after we examined the dynamics of their upbringing along with the present-day circumstances, Tilly was more accepting of this premise. She expressed how sad she felt that this dynamic had infused a tremendous wedge between them. She wondered how and if she might be able to talk this through with Tracy. When she tried, Tracy went ballistic, telling her that she did not care at all about what Tilly has and was appalled that she dare make such farfetched arguments and accusations.

Tracy is not in touch with her feelings of envy; she cannot allow positive things to happen to her as she is always encountering conflict with her successful twin. Tilly realizes that dissociated thoughts are not available for articulation. She has concluded that her basic strategy will be to accept the situation as is. If she wants to have a relationship with her twin, she will have to decide how and if she can tolerate her sister's envious sentiments. Envy obstructs what could be a close and loving relationship. Envy is a spoiler.

Conflict Resolution: Healthy Differentiation

MISSY, AN ADULT identical twin in her fifties, came to see me to help her resolve her contemptuous and irksome feelings toward her twin sister. Missy was ashamed of these thoughts. She had recently spent a few vacation days with her twin and was distressed that she felt so annoyed by her and could not wait for her to leave. Although they lived on different sides of the country, they had always kept in close contact with each other. At the time, they were having more frequent interactions because they were dealing with the care of their elderly mother.

Missy had never been in therapy before and made it clear from the start that she had no intention of having more than a short-term experience. She was a professional woman who had opted not to marry and felt comfortable with her choices and lifestyle. She repeatedly mentioned that she felt very loved by both of her parents. Her father had passed away several years ago. She was adamant that her childhood had been just fine. She scoffed at the idea that her present difficulties might be related to childhood experiences.

Rather than uncover past difficulties, Missy wanted me to help her get rid of her guilty intolerance toward her mother and sister. She felt despicable about expressing anger or resentment toward her mother and twin. She believed that her impatience and small-mindedness were her fault, having nothing to do with her twin's and mother's selfish and inconsiderate reactions. Missy wanted to be less sensitive to or reactive about the ways in which she felt dismissed and devalued by both of them.

In time we explored how she had little capacity to appreciate and manage her ambivalent feelings. In fact, her dissociated anger and hurt had tainted many other intimate relationships. Gradually she understood that being able to acknowledge negative feelings and thoughts did not make her a hateful, ungrateful person. To the contrary, Missy recognized that being able to articulate and own hostile feelings empowered her to embrace a new perspective about the personality traits of her twin and mother.

She realized how different she was from her twin, probably for the first time. Missy had not realized how their sensibilities diverged. So instead of railing against her twin's insensitive parenting style, obsessional thinking, and chronic complaints, Missy let go of these gripes and relaxed, without self-recrimination or a belief that she was obliged to do something about these issues.

In our concluding sessions, Missy talked freely about her very close friend who had recently died. Their relationship had been authentic, reciprocal, and intimate. She could be herself in many ways, including expressing her disappointments and sadness. When Missy was able to appreciate how different she felt with her girlfriend, she felt less triggered and entangled with her twin and mother. Over time she communicated her true feelings with ease and self-acceptance.

True to her word, she ended therapy when she felt her goal had been accomplished. I was absolutely on board with her plan. A patient's agenda in therapy should be heeded and respected first and foremost. We therapists are there to serve our client's needs, not our own.

Boundaries

I RECENTLY SPOKE with several twins whose relationships have been adversely affected and undermined by a lack of proper boundaries. This can be an ordinary consequence of navigating a twin connection. However, when boundaries are improperly managed, twins may have serious difficulty recognizing and eventually reconciling the importance of respecting and acknowledging separateness and space.

An article from the *Journal of Infant, Child, and Adolescent Psychotherapy* entitled "Holding the Line: Limits in Child Psychotherapy" stresses the importance of boundaries:

> Developmental research clarifies children's needs for external limits. Children reared with nurturing yet firm parental guidance generally exhibit the best developmental outcomes, whereas children raised in families in which limits are unnecessarily harsh or overly loose often show emotional and behavioral difficulties. . . . The caregiver's attuned reflection, regulation, and modification of the child's states teach the child to label, tolerate, organize, and manage emotions. Caregivers' containment of children's negative affects enables children to regulate themselves. When caregivers fail to provide such regulation, children's emotions can overwhelm them and lead to feelings of frightful omnipotence or disorganization.

A pair of identical twin men in their fifties are contending with this issue. One called me to help him cope with his sadness and anger about losing his connection with his brother after many tumultuous years of conflict and animosity. According to his account, neither he nor his brother were able to understand why they could not work through their difficulties. Both blamed the other for the rift in their relationship. Their burgeoning differences and disappointments with one another escalated into anger and resentment. Over the last ten years or so, the rift worsened to the point that neither brother feels there is any hope of working things through. In many ways, their situation is akin to a divorce in which both parties are convinced they have little chance of reconciliation.

From what I can piece together, the brothers initially had a very enmeshed and codependent relationship. When one of them needed considerable help, his brother felt good about being able to meet his twin's needs. However, as the years went by, the needs of the cared-for brother changed. While grateful for his brother's ongoing ministrations, he wanted to be more independent. He recognized that he needed to be on his own rather than feel worried or guilty about hurting his brother's feelings if he did not take his brother's advice.

After he started to resist his brother's continued involvement, tensions escalated. His twin felt powerless, diminished, and disappointed about no longer being needed. As a result, he became hostile and even more controlling. Understandably, the caretaking twin felt rejected and devalued by his brother's decreasing need for his support. He felt unappreciated and sad. He had expected the relationship to provide lifelong, unrestricted access to his twin.

The years of acrimony resulting from the brothers' inability to understand each other resulted in a schism that will most likely remain unchanged unless they can muster the desire to establish a new normal in their relationship. For valid reasons, both men feel betrayed, upset, and pessimistic about trying to manage their incompatible personality styles.

I only wish I had had the opportunity to meet with both men earlier in their journey. Both twins and singletons have to put in the work to maintain a connection with their siblings. Being a twin does not automatically ensure an eternally seamless bond.

Duped or Disappointed: A Different End Game

THE OTHER DAY a patient told me that she felt "duped." I asked her to explain what she meant by that. She related that she experienced feeling betrayed or taken advantage of by someone.

As we explored the incident together, it seemed clear in her case that feeling duped felt shameful. Being disappointed by someone appeared less toxic than admitting shame since disappointment does not usually evoke intense feelings of self-loathing and victimization.

Many aspects are at play that may contribute to feeling shame. Those who have studied the intricate aspects of shame link it primarily to a disruption in the relational attachment from a young age. Somewhere along the developmental path, a child and significant others experience a complicated and conflicted relationship, which can result in the child feeling as if she is the cause of "bad" emotional ruptures. A feedback loop of feeling bad, responsible, and rageful can contribute to a shame-based nature, which evolves into self-consciousness and self-loathing.

Among the twin pairs I have treated, shame-based behaviors are an expectable outcome of an unhealthy twin connection. When each twin vies for status, recognition, and validation, one twin may end up feeling less loveable, less valuable, or less important. To manage these uncomfortable circumstances, one twin may disavow her inferior status by becoming the caretaker twin. In so doing, she pathologically accommodates to the needs of her twin and often her mother. As time goes on, the caretaker twin remains in the background, seemingly making way for her twin to shine while she dissociates from the resentment and victimization of the relational inequities. She descends into a pattern of passivity and dependency, further contributing to her sense of despair. She feels inconsequential and secondary, having little to offer in terms of self-agency or self-confidence.

To confront and remedy this situation, a twin in treatment should be encouraged to get in touch with the disavowed rageful and defiant feelings designed to protect herself from feeling shame. While singletons may have to work through this dynamic in their relationships, it is doubly difficult for twins to navigate this terrain. The loyalty siblings "owe" their twin demands a conformity that further erodes individuality.

If we can feel sorry for ourselves and experience an authentic flash of self-pity, we can begin to acknowledge our situation without shame or debilitating regret. Anticipating change is undeniably difficult. Yet having the courage to recognize one's vulnerability is tantamount to developing the confidence to embrace hope, positivity, and free will.

Why Do Separations Feel Like Abandonments?

RESEARCH ON ATTACHMENT consistently shows that our experiences with our parents influence how we raise our own children. Many twin pairs had minimal parental connections and consequently had to "parent" each other.

I have worked for many months with an identical twin in her forties. Two ongoing issues prompted her to get in touch with me: a longstanding rift with her twin and the tumultuous, treacherous behavior of her then seventeen-year-old son. At that point, she did not understand that the adolescent boy was acting out partially because he needed to break away from her. Eventually, he left her house and moved in with his father, who had separated from my client many years before.

Fern told me that separations feel like desertions. She has experienced this reaction with her twin sister and with her sons. She grew up in a violent household where she felt unloved and victimized by her parents and older sisters. Only her twin relationship offered any support or solace. So after her twin married, she felt utterly alone and desolate. With a sense of urgency, she married a man similar to her twin's spouse.

Fern emotionally smothered her boys. At the same time, she was wildly envious that her sister gave birth to two daughters. She described her connection with her younger son as "beyond enmeshment." She said, "I can look into his eyes, feel what he feels, and know what he's thinking. I am my son." In return for her sacrifice and devotion, she demanded that her sons mirror her particular cultural beliefs and expectations. She told me that loving parents should be worshipped for their assiduous care and support.

When her twenty-five-year-old son announced that he planned to move into an apartment with some friends, Fern reacted with rage and disbelief: "How can he do this to me?" His decision to leave home and separate from her felt like an insufferable narcissistic blow that announced to the whole world that she was a bad mother. She declared that children who do not live at home to save money are breaking the rules of engagement.

As one might imagine, helping Fern understand and appreciate the role that separation plays in healthy development has been challenging. Our work together focuses on how her traumatic upbringing thwarted her ability to become a separate person. Her overreliance on her twin was a consequence of sadistic parenting. Her sister's desire to disconnect from Fern stemmed from a need to feel independent. Prior to counseling, Fern could not fathom why her sister deserted her. She surmised that the separation meant that Fern was unlovable, unattractive, and too boisterous. As a result, she was flooded with rage and self-loathing—the only two emotions she recognized and vehemently enacted.

In truth, until one safely grows into feeling like a separate individual, separations will be experienced as betrayals and desertions.

What Did You Ever Do for Me?

I WORK WITH A PAIR of identical twin women whose individual temperaments are as diverse as night and day. One of the twins, Sue, is a school nurse, and the other, Ellen, crunches numbers at a food warehouse business. Much of the focus of our work has been articulating the differences in the way they think, feel, and approach life. At times, Sue becomes frustrated when she expresses her needs and feelings because Ellen has difficulty grasping abstract concepts such as mirroring and codependency.

A recent session was most interesting in that it highlighted so beautifully how difficult it is for twins of all ages and types to manage feelings related to inequality or disparity. More than ten years ago, Ellen suffered an acute depressive episode related to her family's unwillingness to support her financially at the college of her choice. Even though the family members participated in family therapy, Ellen felt as if her sister and her family had let her down. Ellen recalled that the therapy concentrated on her outward symptoms of anxiety and depression without actually getting at the real issues. Ellen sobs uncontrollably each and every time she talks about this traumatic time in her life. While she says she has moved on from it, she clearly has not been able to do so.

This same matter surfaced once again when Sue brought up how hurt and angry she felt the other day about Ellen's inability to affirm her distraught feelings about a family member. Sue complained that it is difficult to feel connected to Ellen because Ellen cannot validate her feelings. Ellen habitually responds to her sister's emotional rants with dismissive comments and useless strategies. This time, in response or in retaliation, Ellen answered that she could not honestly respond to her sister's intense emotional feelings because she did not agree with them; consequently, she felt an "incongruity" within herself. Undoubtedly, she is often so defensively focused on her own distress that she cannot listen or respond to Sue's feelings with either empathy or affirmation.

Sue listened intently to Ellen's dilemma about not being able to respond authentically to her feelings. At that moment, Ellen started to sob again and said that it's all unfair. She asked, "Why should I empathize with Sue's feelings when she did nothing for me when I needed help?" Sue explained apologetically that she was not psychologically capable at that time to respond more appropriately. She was enmeshed with her parents and felt she had no other choice than to accommodate their wishes.

I mentioned how difficult it is for twins to manage these kinds of issues because their families and society at large compare twins throughout their lives. Many twin pairs struggle much more than singletons and their siblings because of the twin mystique. The expectation that they should be best friends and soul mates forever makes it almost impossible for twins to process their feelings of anger, envy, frustration, and resentment. I hope that my ongoing efforts will help educate more and more people about the healthy outcomes associated with twins' capacity to work through feelings they are not "supposed" to have.

Tilting at Windmills

MANY PSYCHOTHERAPISTS feel disheartened and discouraged when treating a couple who appear unable to reestablish trust and stability. A similar situation occurs with twin pairs who struggle to get their relationship back on track. Working through upsetting events and traumatic feelings requires a tremendous amount of effort, dedication, and commitment.

I am helping a pair of identical female twins in their midfifties listen to one another more effectively and rekindle their connection. A number of complex variables hindered the evolution of their relationship for many years. Since their mother died a year ago, both sisters recognize that the only family they have left is each other. Feeling desperate because of their inability to get along and recognize each other as separate people, they contacted me for help.

Both women have diametrically opposing personalities, which is one of many factors contributing to their lack of connection. Sally is outspoken, energetic, fast paced, and extroverted. Her sister Serena is methodical, low key, shy, and orderly. When something that her sister says or does upsets Serena, she shuts down completely. She becomes anxious when she hears Sally express frustration, anger, or impatience; consequently, she cannot respond to Sally's feelings in any meaningful way. Serena shared that it took her two years to muster up the courage to tell Sally that she hated visiting Sally's apartment because it was so messy and unkempt.

Sally, on the other hand, doesn't understand why Serena cannot respond to her feelings at all. Since Sally believes that she expresses her feelings in a clear and concise manner, she becomes distraught over Serena's inability to take care of her in these moments. Sally also panics when Serena thwarts her efforts to be Serena's emotional caretaker. Sally played this role throughout their lives and feels stripped of her function when Serena rejects her offers of advice and counsel. Telephone conversations between the sisters become empty and meaningless because Serena's need for quiet self-reflection and passive responses leave Sally feeling empty, alone, and abandoned.

Both women endured tremendous emotional and physical trauma growing up. As a result, Sally has adopted a persona that comes across as dogmatic, controlling, and powerful. Serena, on the other hand, says that she never felt heard or recognized in her family because Sally was the stronger twin. As a result, Serena is reluctant to assert herself in any real way when her sister is involved. She reverts back to her childhood, feeling isolated and alone in her attempts to handle overwhelming fears. The sisters long to feel safe and loved by each other but are tragically paralyzed by old defensive patterns. Both are understandably fearful of changing themselves or trusting each other, so they hide their vulnerability behind their childhood roles. Their interpersonal difficulties spill over into other relationships outside of their twin connection. Both look for friends who can mirror exactly what they need to feel safe and recognized.

My therapeutic goal for Sally and Serena is to tackle the traumatic childhood experiences that continue to drive a wedge between the sisters, which hopefully will establish a safe emotional place for each of them. If they can agree to disagree and find a place of mutual recognition, each will be able to work through their emotional distress—Sally will allow Serena to be herself, and Serena will learn how to manage Sally's wrath without fear of incrimination or retaliation.

The title of this essay refers to the notion that many of us, not just twins, deplete ourselves emotionally by fighting outdated psychic demons that continue to haunt us. Psychoanalytic psychotherapy enables the patient to understand the developmental root causes of presenting issues and work toward a healthier resolution in the future.

Communicating as Two Separate People

MARTHA, A YOUNG WOMAN in her thirties, grew up in a volatile household. Her twin, Marsha, was her security, safety, and protection from an abusive mother and nasty older sisters. Martha was devoted to her twin and never entertained the notion that one day Marsha would want or need space from her. This unexpected predicament occurred after they graduated from high school. Martha had assumed they would live together and attend the same university. So she was completely taken off guard when these expectations did not materialize. Martha related that she was deeply depressed during her college years as she felt alone and abandoned.

Eventually, both women married and pursued their independent careers. Yet Martha never fully recovered from the separation. The twins' communication lessened considerably over time. Martha sought treatment because she was desperate to reconnect with Marsha but was stymied by feelings of fear, betrayal, and anger.

Martha described a pattern of relating that happened frequently when she did speak to Marsha. Marsha would begin the conversation by talking about herself. When Martha tried to participate in the conversation and share things about her life, she felt that Marsha seemed disinterested and distracted. At the slightest hint of this misattunement, Martha went into emotional overdrive. She described it to me as follows:

- She did not hear what I said.
- She is self-centered and preoccupied.
- She does not care about me.
- She is competing with me.
- I am enraged with her.
- I need her to need me.
- I feel like a vulnerable, disgusting, unlovable person who will be abandoned again.

Eventually, owing in large part to their separate individual psychotherapy, each woman developed the emotional capability and safety to be able to say how the other's behavior made her feel. In fact, they decided to use a certain code word to signal that one or both were feeling hurt and needed to be heard. Perhaps this is their love language—the way they can alert each other as to how they feel and then navigate through the distressed feelings to arrive at some sort of mutual understanding.

This strategy can work if both twins feel like separate individuals who can listen to the perspective of another as well as take responsibility for their feelings. If not, the conversation will just become a useless blame game where neither person can feel like a winner or be heard.

Part VII

TWIN LOSS AND ESTRANGEMENT

THE LOSS OF A TWIN cannot be adequately understood in the context of a singleton's grief over the loss of a sibling. When a twin bond has existed throughout one's life, the surviving twin often feels as if a part of them has died with their twin. In fact, many twins are plagued with the sense "when my twin died, I died too," given that they have lost the person they felt closest to and loved the most. For the bereaved twin, shared memories, experiences, feelings, and connections seem to be lost forever without the living presence of their deceased sibling. Unfortunately, many twins relate that their prolonged grief after having lost their twin is experienced by others as pathological. They describe how they are often met with the unstated question: "Why are you not over this yet?"

In this section are stories from twins coping with various issues following the death of their beloved twin. For example, one of my patients reported that she felt as if half of herself had vanished, partly because her connection to her brother had always given her a sense of purpose and well-being. She wondered how she would be able to make a life for herself without the best friend, supportive partner, and soul mate he had always been for her. Like others experiencing twin loss, she will have to learn to foster other adult relationships, which she may have had little incentive to do when her twin was alive. Twin loss and its attendant depression, grief, and loneliness are exacerbated when the surviving twin hasn't fully developed a separate self.

The death of a twin is not the only circumstance in which one experiences twin loss. There is another type of twin loss that occurs when one or both twins decide to completely cut off contact with the other. The resulting sense of loss can be as devastating as a death. One twin may become estranged from the other for a variety of reasons. The twin who chooses to permanently separate may have longstanding grievances or a more immediate one that justifies breaking off the relationship. He may feel so disillusioned or annoyed with aspects of the twin connection that he's compelled to go his own way and have nothing to do with the other twin. When a twinship is broken in this way, the loss is indeed felt as a death. Healing from such a loss will involve an openness to a deeper understanding of one's twinship issues.

Twin Loss: Tragic and Terrifying

I HAVE BEEN WORKING with a middle-aged woman whose twin brother died suddenly and unexpectedly a few years ago. It has taken her a long time to find the right therapist to help her work through her loss.

She tried attending various grief groups; however, her disappointment and anger about not finding anyone who could intrinsically understand the loss as it related to the twin relationship made the process all the more difficult, painful, and prolonged. She appreciated email exchanges with members of the internet group Twinless Twins (twinlesstwins.org); nonetheless, she needed to relate directly to a person rather than attempt to work through her grieving process via virtual connections.

I have read most of the literature about twin loss. The seminal work about the subject is a book called *The Lone Twin* written by Joan Woodward in 1998. Woodward is a well-respected British psychotherapist who was drawn to the issue of twin loss because her identical twin sister died at three years of age. She came to recognize that her psychoanalytic training and treatment paid no attention and lent little importance to this very significant life event. She researched the stages of twin loss at various developmental ages and described them in her book.

Helping my patient work through the loss of her brother has highlighted the complexities of twin attachments. My patient feels as if half of herself has vanished. Her connection to her brother imbued her with a sense of purpose and being. They were best friends, supportive partners, and soul mates. They helped each other in all sorts of ways: they loaned each other money; they gave each other rides when one of them did not have a car; they shared holidays, rituals, and their birthdays; they supported each other in their recoveries from addictions. Both of them felt unconditionally loved by the other. In the face of their individual struggles, they remained present, protective, and proactive for each another.

In this emotional atmosphere, one can surely appreciate how lonely and sad my patient feels—at times contemplating suicide and at other times feeling guilty that she is alive and he is not. She is learning how to live and to survive without him—a formidable task given how much they meant to each other. She was blessed to have her brother in her life; however, without him, she feels cursed by her loneliness and dependence, wondering how she will be able to make a life for herself without him. While the notion of creating a life after the death of a loved one is a daunting task in most cases, how much more difficult must it be to lose an attachment created in utero?

Flying Solo

I HAVE HAD THE PRIVILEGE of helping Meredith, a middle-aged twin woman, reclaim herself following the sudden loss of her twin brother. When her brother died unexpectedly, her world fell apart. Both twins had been heavily emotionally dependent on one another in a myriad of complex and complicated ways.

At two years of age, their father took Meredith and her brother away from their biological mother because she was too mentally unstable to care for them. He subsequently remarried, and the twins were raised by a stern, controlling stepmother. Meredith and her brother clung to one another for emotional support throughout their childhood. When they went different ways at eighteen, they remained in constant contact. They saw one another frequently; they rescued one another from financial difficulties; and they staunchly relied upon one another to get through uncomfortable family gatherings. Meredith relied on her brother like a parent, sibling, and best friend. His death robbed her of the only person she had ever truly loved or trusted. His absence left an emotional void that kept her depressed, immobilized, and drug addicted for many months.

As Meredith has emerged from her mourning and sadness, she has grown into the persona that her brother embraced. This transformative shift has helped her feel empowered, enabling her to incorporate many of the functions and strengths that he had habitually provided for her. She has become more adult, mature, and responsible. She is doing for herself what her brother used to do for her—acting as a compassionate other, celebrating her growth and successes, and sustaining a more independent and positive outlook on life. In many ways, she seems reborn as an individual who embodies the best qualities of both her brother and herself.

She recognizes these changes in herself, cherishing memories, stories, and experiences about their twin connection. She is attempting to foster other adult relationships, which she had little incentive to do when her brother was alive. By embracing the love, concern, and compassion that her brother showered her with throughout their lives together, she is integrating self-love and self-esteem for herself. This was not conceivable when her brother was alive because they provided one another with a shared strength. Now, fending for herself, she is becoming a strong woman trying to learn how to navigate emotional ups and downs without her better half—and succeeding quite well.

The Vicissitudes of Twin Loss

In the last few months, I have been working with two grieving families. In both instances, a fraternal twin died owing to accidental circumstances—a drug overdose in one family and an automobile collision in the other. The man was in his late thirties and the young woman in her late twenties.

While my heart goes out to those who have lost a loved one, I am inclined to be most concerned about the surviving twins and their well-being. In both cases, the surviving twin was the caretaker in the twin relationship. Each family has described in detail how involved and invested each surviving twin was in the life of the deceased sibling. Each twin had devoted considerable years to the direct care of his or her twin.

The surviving male twin, Alex, spent almost all of his young adulthood looking out for his brother, Teddy. Alex is focused and ambitious, while Teddy appeared more easygoing and engaging.

The boys' mother died when they were young teens. Their lives became disorganized and chaotic following her death. While Alex was able to get back on his feet toward the end of their high school years, Teddy struggled with alcohol and drugs. Teddy experienced short-lived periods of health and prosperity; however, he repeatedly fell on hard times and reverted back to using drugs and alcohol.

Alex was ready and willing to drop whatever he was doing and come to Teddy's aid. At times Alex moved closer to Teddy; other times Teddy would move into Alex's apartment until he felt able to be on his own again.

Alex recalls that he heard from Teddy the night before his death. At that time Teddy had moved into a nearby apartment with his girlfriend. They spoke every day, and Alex remained vigilant about checking on Teddy's whereabouts and safety.

Alex's preoccupation with Teddy's emotional and physical security inhibited and prevented Alex from having his own life. Up to the time of Teddy's death, Alex had not pursued his own intimate connections. While he worked hard and had many workplace friends, Alex's primary emotional investment was in Teddy.

Understandably, Alex has been stricken with remorse and sadness since his brother's death. Alex continues to feel that he could have saved Teddy if only he had detected that something was amiss during their last conversation.

A very similar set of dynamics existed for Emily, the young woman whose twin sister, Elaine, passed away unexpectedly in an auto accident. Emily, the surviving twin, was the "mother hen" and felt defined by her role as Elaine's best friend. In fact, Emily's feelings of self-worth and fulfillment originated from Elaine's dependence on Emily. Robbed of this job, function, and identity of being Elaine's one and only, Emily now struggles to find her own sense of self amid terrific emotions of guilt, remorse, and anger.

While loss of any sort is tragic, please pay special attention to twin loss. It cannot be understood within the context of a singleton's grief over the loss of a sibling. It is simply not the same. The surviving twin's age at the time of the other twin's death and their relational dynamic will be of great significance in terms of defining future developmental milestones and emotional maturity. However, in view of the twin bond that has existed throughout their lives, twins often feel as if a part of themselves has died with their twin.

The grief and mourning process is long and arduous. For surviving twins to regain and redefine an identity after this traumatic event, they must work toward developing an identity that encompasses more than just forever being a twin.

Twin Loss:
An Epigenetic Accident

Cathy, a woman in her early twenties, wrote me a beautiful email asking for advice about how to deal with the loss of her twin. She explained that she had read my book *The Same but Different* and found it helpful in many ways; however, her circumstances were such that my book could not offer her the specific help she needed. She hoped I would be able to provide additional resources for her after I learned more about her particular circumstances.

Cathy and her identical twin sister, Connie, grew up in a rural town in the South. They did everything together and were essentially inseparable. Close to the end of their freshman year in college, Connie experienced her first full-blown manic episode. She was hospitalized, diagnosed with bipolar disorder, and prescribed medication.

Up to that point, Connie's behavior seemed relatively normal. Nonetheless, Cathy recalled two incidents that occurred in high school and perhaps foreshadowed things to come. Once, Connie inexplicably hid a pair of tennis shoes that belonged to a girl on their tennis team. The team hunted for the shoes and ultimately found that Connie had thrown them in a trash can. Cathy also remembered walking into the art classroom and discovering that Connie had ripped her own final art project to shreds and put the pieces in a plastic bag.

Without consulting her twin sister, Cathy decided to attend a junior college near their hometown. At the last minute, Connie decided to join her. They lived together in a campus dorm. However, after the first bipolar episode, their relationship rapidly deteriorated. Connie did not comply with her medications, and her behavior was erratic and unpredictable. Connie accused Cathy of not being adequately concerned about her, and Cathy's parents also expected Cathy to take care of her sister. No other family member wanted to bear the responsibility of Connie's difficult circumstances.

Cathy described what transpired a year ago in detail. Connie burst into Cathy's apartment one afternoon. She threw Cathy against the wall, pushed her down on the kitchen floor, and beat her mercilessly. Fortunately, a neighbor heard the commotion and called the police. Connie was hospitalized in a psychiatric facility for a short time and then released. Cathy has not seen her sister since this incident. She does not return Connie's texts or telephone calls and wants nothing more to do with her.

Cathy misses Connie—the twin sister who was her best friend and trusted companion—terribly. Cathy remains traumatized by what happened and fearful about the future. We talked about the organization Twinless Twins, whose primary purpose is to help people who have lost their twin to an illness, an accident, or suicide. What makes Cathy's predicament so sad is that her sister is alive but not well. I suggested that perhaps it would be helpful to view her situation as losing her twin to the epigenetic accident of bipolar disorder.

Cathy remarked that she had relied on Connie to initiate social interactions. She explained that Connie made the friends and Cathy kept them. Cathy was having difficulty navigating this challenge alone. We discussed some cognitive strategies to help her feel more comfortable on her own in social settings.

Did I Make My Twin Crazy?

IT BREAKS MY HEART when I speak to an identical twin whose sibling has a psychiatric disorder. In addition to the healthy twin's distress and sadness about her sibling's state of mind, she often believes that she somehow contributed to her sister's mental condition. Most of the twins I have worked with experience an enormous sense of guilt and shame over their sibling's psychological disturbance.

The healthy twin can identify specific experiences where her sister may have felt resentful of her relationship or career successes. Or she may recall how she and her twin competed in looks and popularity. The underlying issues of envy and jealousy weigh heavily on the "victor" as a punishment for triumphing over her twin.

Interestingly, in most of the cases where I am directly involved, the psychiatric diagnoses are clear—manic depressive disorder, borderline personality, and drug and alcohol addiction. Naturally, identical twins have difficulty understanding why one twin is afflicted and the other is not. They know that they have the exact same DNA—so how does this happen? At this point, I explain the importance of epigenetic influences on the development of illness in one twin and not the other.

Even more upsetting is the fact that many twins acted as parental surrogates for each other. Thus, their reactions of guilt and failure feel akin to those of parents who grapple with a child's mental difficulties. Unfortunately, incessant negative and dangerous interactions with one's ill twin can damage the twinship beyond repair. On one hand, the healthy twin is relieved that the deteriorating connection is severed, but on the other hand, she remains terribly sad and bereft, mourning the passing of the beautiful moments of her special relationship with her sibling.

The loss of a still-living twin is profound. Helping the healthier twin to acknowledge her ambivalence about her sister's condition and to accept that she is not responsible for it is an ongoing process. She must eventually recognize that she tried her best to help her twin in the face of serious emotional and physical harm. Sometimes, one can do little besides accept the sad reality of the situation and work through feelings of blame, helplessness, and defeat.

Twins: Siblings Cut from a Different Cloth

JANET, A COLLEAGUE of mine, who lost her identical twin to cancer about four years ago, shared some interesting insights after she attended a sibling grief group. She has participated in several twinless-twin groups for many years. As a professional interested in learning more about her loss, she became curious about how nontwin siblings experience and manage their grief.

An important backstory is that Janet and her sister, like many other twin pairs, grew up without adequate maternal attention. Janet described that she and her sister acted as surrogate parents for each other. She was the caretaking twin who dedicated herself to her sister's emotional and physical well-being from the beginning to the end of her twin's ongoing medical challenges, which stretched more than twenty-five years.

Even before her sister passed away, my colleague recognized that she would need to find a therapist to help her prepare for and cope with her twin's death as well as address how the loss of her sister would impact her fragile identity. She knew living without her twin was imminent. Nevertheless, through force of habit, her waking thoughts and life decisions were inextricably tied to her relationship with her twin.

Janet related that the sibling loss group highlighted a few major differences from her twinless-twin experiences. First, she was surprised by how nontwin siblings in the grief group were involved with others, including parents and other siblings. She explained that her twin loss experiences underscored how often twins are distant from their parents and other family members. For that reason she describes twinless twins as "forgotten mourners." Many twin families are confused and angry in times of loss because they don't understand the complexity and interdependency of the twinship. Calling attention to some significant differences between twin siblings and nontwin siblings adds an important dimension in our ongoing quest to help twins and their families manage loss and grief.

Twin Loss: A Double Dose of Grief

Many twins will tell you that losing a twin is unlike sibling loss. The depth and power of the twin bond that has grown over a lifetime cannot be duplicated by any other intimate connection.

Their lives of shared experiences—both positive and negative—are embedded in their collective DNA.

I was speaking a few days ago to a young man in his thirties whose identical twin passed away about a month ago. His death was unexpected in the sense that his cancer had been in remission. I had spoken via Zoom a few times with him and his brother during the COVID-19 pandemic. The issue they were grappling with at that time had to do with being able to recognize and respect that each of them had personality differences that contributed to relationship tension from time to time. Since one young man was a bit more outgoing than the other, they worked at giving one another space without hurting the other's feelings. Simply put, their differences did not become divisive because their communication about these different needs was shared and respected. In fact, getting to the heart of this issue enabled both to be more honest and authentic about their specific wishes.

The surviving twin is understandably bereft. He relates that there is no one else in his life who knew everything about him—that precious gift to know someone instantly and deeply.

He talked about his identity. He is a twin and always will be, but how does one become accustomed to being a twinless twin? Fortunately, he has many other friends, family members, and personal and professional obligations that help him stay busy and engaged in life.

He said that he felt very fortunate that they had worked through their minor emotional difficulties. While he can be at peace about that, he is suffering the deep traumatic loss of his brother and their connection. The twin bond is irreplaceable.

When Twins Break Up

TWINS WHO DO NOT get along with their sibling definitely feel a sense of loss. Although the rupture most likely begins with anger and resentment, the ultimate split results in a distressing emotional upheaval. While this estrangement is not tantamount to the death of one's twin, the split can nonetheless intensify painful feelings of grief and regret. Acknowledging that one's twin connection is no longer special or comforting is heartbreaking. In fact, some twins feel tremendous shame over the split.

One twin may become estranged from the other for a variety of reasons. The twin who chooses to separate usually has either long-standing grievances or a more immediate one that justifies breaking off the relationship. One twin may feel disillusioned or fed up with aspects of the twin connection; his inability to work things out with the sibling leads to blame, defiance, and self-righteousness.

A split is often precipitated by one twin's relationship with an intimate other. The third party disrupts the dyadic safety net. For example, a partner, spouse, or significant other may become frustrated with being second rate or second best. Unfortunately, the loyalty conflicts that ensue have no easy solution. A split may not be amenable to repair or resolution. In these situations, the "twinless twins" are left to process and adjust to this painful loss on their own.

Estrangement Can Make You Feel Like a Twinless Twin

WHEN WE HEAR ABOUT a twinless twin, we likely associate that description with someone whose twin has passed away. Nonetheless, some people who are estranged from their same-age sibling can also feel like twinless twins even though their sibling is still very much alive. Since much of my work revolves around twin pairs who struggle to reconnect or who must come to terms with being estranged, it feels apt to acknowledge that one can feel like a twinless twin when the relationship with one's sibling is broken or nonexistent.

As I have written previously, twins who do not get along feel like social pariahs and apologetic failures. Not living up to the stereotypic expectation that twins must be best friends and soul mates contributes to their embarrassment. Their sense of shame and self-loathing can be intense and deep rooted, growing out of the powerfully close relationship that defined them for so many years.

Those who no longer regard their twin as their best friend have a steep learning curve. Twins grow apart for many sensible, plausible, and expectable reasons. Perhaps if public opinion did not hold them to such absurd, idealistic standards, more twin pairs might be capable of separating emotionally and developing a new intimacy based on adult behaviors.

Feeling the freedom to make one's own decisions and choices without incurring pushback, guilt, or resentment from one's twin would definitely help to ameliorate the rivalry and hostility that can lead to twins misunderstanding one another. Learning to view disagreements as two dissenting opinions instead of a breach in the relationship would minimize feelings of abandonment. Unfortunately, emotional rifts can lead to physical separations and acrimonious discord, which are sometimes irreparable.

The process of grieving the loss of one's twin can become seriously convoluted if the surviving sibling has unresolved feelings, conscious or unconscious, about his twin connection. Perhaps he was never able to articulate or understand some of the complexities of the twinship. Grief counselors tell us that having closure with a loved one who passed away helps to mitigate the agonizing loss and sadness. Since many twin relationships remain shrouded in childhood constructs, alienated twins may have difficulty working through unresolved issues. Usually, they lacked opportunities to access and understand the hidden, unrecognized difficulties embedded in their relationship. Perhaps having exposure to the complexities of healthy twin development would ease the ongoing process of grief.

Grudges, Guilt, and Grief: The Facets of Twin Estrangement

THE INABILITY OF TWINS to get along has many possible explanations—for example, complications with a twin's significant other, a twin's mental illness or emotional instability, unabated competitive rivalry, parental favoritism of one twin over the other. What underlies all these issues is the siblings' profound grief and sadness about the loss of their twinness. Their shared childhood fantasies and aspirations are shattered. These imagined scenarios and hopes cannot be fulfilled by anyone else.

One young woman sobbed inconsolably about not fulfilling her dream of shopping for her bridal gown with her twin sister. As children they had invented fantasies and played out countless plans about their growing up together. Often these thoughts would include marrying twins, living next door to each other, and being a mother to each other's children. When twins read about this actually happening to a few select twin pairs, they envy and admire this possibility.

However, as life evolves and disparities occur, some dreams inevitably fade. There is no replacement for one's twin. The ongoing unraveling and devastation of the siblings' mutual dreams and desires may reach a breaking point. They cannot find their way back because there is none. They must forcibly let go of their childhood wishes. Frequently they blame each other for the ending of their blissful run.

Either one or both twins end up feeling shortchanged or cheated out of their happy ending.

Having relied on each other for mirroring and validation, they are lost after the rupture as they struggle to find support elsewhere. They are panic stricken and overwhelmed, desperate in some cases to reconnect to feel some modicum of familiar stability once again. Or they must forge ahead to create and develop alternative ways of connecting to others to establish new attachments. Sadly, many twin pairs are ill equipped to do so because they are inexperienced in managing conflict and accepting differences.

Their disparities contribute to their feelings of disconnection and abandonment because they have missed opportunities to develop self-reflective capacities. Having grown up with a shared self rather than a separate self impedes twins' capacity to embrace and accept divergent perceptions and experiences that do not mirror the other's thinking or beliefs. Sadly, they cannot be *real* twins if they disagree.

Accept Reality and Move On

THE NOTION OF ACCEPTING a less than desired outcome is a difficult lesson and a bitter pill to swallow. Often we strive to make things or have things go in the direction that we desire. This idea can apply to relationships of all kinds as well as to decisions we make about spending money, redecorating our home, or buying a car. We do our best to live with whatever consequences may result.

So it goes with making peace with your twin. I have counseled many twin couples who are upset because they are not getting along as well as they had hoped or expected. Their adult roles and responsibilities have added burdensome issues that have interfered with their expectations for closeness and reciprocity. These same conflicts can emerge in partnerships of all sorts. Yet twins do expect an enormous payoff.

Many twins express frustration and sadness about their unhappy twin connection. Gradually, however, as they begin to talk about their childhood and their perspectives, they begin to recognize the significant differences between them. When they can get to the point of understanding that their differences make them more capable of getting along rather than alienating them, they can experience a breakthrough in their attachment. They can develop a more tolerant and respectful attitude toward each other.

If you want your twin in your life, at some point you might need to admit a few things to yourself:

- My relationship with my twin is not as close as I would like it to be or how it used to be.
- My twin is not interested in or capable of talking things through with me.
- I am disappointed and long for a closer connection with my twin.
- I struggle to accept compromise because I miss our idealized bond.

Identicality cannot always sustain twinship glue.

Conclusion

THE WRITINGS IN THIS book have emphasized what I believe are the most effective approaches to parenting twins and understanding twin psychology: making a concerted, ongoing effort to attach to each child rather than to the pair as a unit and letting go of the self-imposed obligation to make everything in the twins' lives fair and equal. Parents' discomfort with inequalities sets the stage for the belief that one twin's life will always be the same as the other's. This expectation leaves the siblings unprepared for their adult transitions and ill equipped to manage the conflicts that will inevitably arise.

If you are a twin, you likely have felt a taboo against talking about not getting along with your twin. Understandable and expectable challenges confront twins as they grow up. These are inevitable and solvable conflicts that accompany developmental changes. They involve patterns of behaviors and dilemmas that twins have not, as yet, had the opportunities to reconcile, including separation, identity confusion, romantic attachments, single friendships, and caretaking issues.

In particular, your teenage years can bring about big changes in your twinship. As you are defining yourself as an individual, do not make the mistake of suppressing your yearning to be seen, appreciated, and valued for your own uniqueness.

If you are the parent of twins, try to spend one-on-one time with each twin to facilitate a healthy recognition of each child's personality and traits, and don't rely on the twins to be surrogate parents for one another. Individual attention can help mitigate the utilization of labels and stereotypes. Also understand that having different feelings for each child is expectable and normal.

If you are the aunt, uncle, or grandparent of twins, try to spend some alone time with each twin. This gift of exclusive time and attention is immeasurable. It's not something twins get very much of and when they do, they feel special and singular. You are making that incredibly rare occurrence happen and additionally enjoying the intimate interaction that accompanies these shared times together.

If you are a mental health clinician or teacher, I urge you to broaden your understanding about a patient or student who happens to be a twin. Expand your emotional awareness and appreciate how growing up as a twin may have affected the person's ability to be resilient and prepared for life as a singleton.

For those who would like more help in fostering a healthier generation of twin pairs, here are a few recommended resources.

Local and Regional Groups

Local and regional groups for parents of twins can provide unparalleled support and camaraderie as parents are adjusting to life with young twins, which is a daunting and exhausting task. For a group in your area, see the Multiples of America website (multiplesofamerica.org).

Social Media, Podcasts, and Websites

I offer helpful videos on my Instagram page. You can find me @dr.joanfriedmantwinexpert.

Several podcasts focus on twins, such as Christine Stewart-Fitzgerald's *Twin Talks*.

The Twinful Life website (twinfullife.com) offers information to support the parents of twins.

Books

You can find many great books for children, such as these two:

- *Take Two!: A Celebration of Twins* by J. Patrick Lewis and Jane Yolen
- *Twin Tales: Hand in Hand across the World* by Elizabeth A. Stewart

As for books for parents, check out any of the following:

- *The Twin Enigma* by Vivienne Lewin
- *Parent Like a Triplet* by Karl Ertresvåg
- *Multiples Illuminated* by Megan Woolsey and Allison Lee
- *Twin Dilemmas* by Barbara Klein
- *What to Do When You're Having Two* by Natalie Diaz

Organizations

The following organizations offer support to families with multiples: International Council of Multiple Births Organization (ICOMBO), Twiniversity, Twins Trust, and Multiples of America.

I urge you to take advantage of these and other available resources.

Helping your twins become their best selves—or, if you are a twin, reaching your own full potential, while also recognizing the differences between siblings and maintaining a good relationship takes work. But no matter the developmental stage, it's never too late for interventions and treatment. I wish you success in your journey.

Index

acceptance, 155–156
adolescent twins
   addressing issues with, 31–32
   bickering between, 33–36
   caretaking behaviors and, 61–62
   fighting between, 41–42
   friends and, 37–38, 43–44
   individuation and, 29–30, 157
   rebelliousness and, 29
   separating, 34, 36, 37–38, 42
   snitching and, 39–40
   social exclusion and, 43–44
attachment theory, 123

betrayal, feelings of, 95–97, 104, 121, 124
bickering, 33–36
Birksted-Breen, Dana, 6–7
birth, mother's feelings after, 5–7
books, 159
boundaries, lack of, 118–120

caretaking behaviors
   coming to terms with roles in, 57–58
   effects of, 44, 45–46, 61–62
   enmeshment and, 50
   examples of, 47–48, 55–56
   origins of, 59
   overly dependent, 49–50, 59–62, 79–80
   parental attention and, 51–52
   school and, 19
caretaking syndrome, 19
clothing, 18
codependency, 34, 55–56, 79–80, 105
comfort zone, finding and leaving, 89–90
comparisons, 19, 107–108
competitiveness, 83–84, 107–110
conflict resolution, 116–117

death of a twin
   effects of, 133–134
   grief and, 136–138, 141, 146–147
   significance of, 133, 135–136, 139–141, 147–149
   transformation after, 137–138
disappointment, 121
dissociation, during pregnancy, 8–9

emotional entitlement, 69–70
enmeshment, 50, 124
envy, 113–115. *See also* jealousy

INDEX

estrangement
   acceptance and, 155–156
   causes of, 134, 150, 153
   effects of, 151–154
   grief and, 150, 152, 153

friends, making, 15–16, 24–25, 37–38, 43–44, 85–86

gift giving, 10–12
grief
   on death of a twin, 136–138, 141, 146–147
   estrangement and, 150, 152, 153

individuation
   adolescent twins and, 29–30, 157
   young adult twins and, 65–66, 71–74
   young twins and, 14, 24
insight, as gateway to change, 98
intimate relationships
   effects of, on nonattached twin, 87–88, 93–97, 104–105
   emotional entitlement and, 70
   impact of twinship on, 88, 90, 91–92, 98–103
   personality traits and, 102–103

jealousy, 83, 113. *See also* envy

marital relationships. *See* intimate relationships
monoamniotic twins, 77
motherhood, as individualized journey, 9

older adult twins
   boundaries and, 118–120
   communication between, as separate people, 130–131
   competitiveness and, 107–110
   conflict and, 109–112, 116–117
   differences between, 111–112, 116–117, 125–126, 148, 155
   envy and, 113–115
   identity and, 109–110
   psychotherapy and, 127–129
   resentments and, 109
   separations and, 123–124, 130–131
organizations, 159
overaccommodation, 66

parenting. *See also* adolescent twins; young twins
   as acquired skill, 13
   bickering and, 33–36
   caretaking behaviors and, 51–52, 61–62
   challenges of, 3–4, 75–76
   effective approaches to, 157–158
   gift giving and, 10–12
   labeling and, 75
   personality types and, 13–14
   postnatal blues and, 5–7
   resources for, 158–159
   school and, 17–19, 23–25
   setting limits and, 13–14
   support groups for, 158
podcasts, 158
postnatal blues, 5–7

pregnancy, dissociation during, 8–9
psychiatric disorders, 142–145

Raphael-Leff, Joan, 6–7
resilience, creating, 89
romantic relationships. *See* intimate relationships

Safer, Jeanne, 20, 21
school
    caretaking syndrome and, 19
    clothing for, 18
    comparisons and, 19
    educating teachers, 18
    separating twins at, 17, 18, 23–25
    starting, 17
self-reliance, 63–64
shame, 121–122
Shusterman, Neal, 89
snitching, 39–40
social media, 158–159
special needs, children with, 20–22

triangulation, 67–68
Twinless Twins, 135, 143
twins. *See also* adolescent twins; older adult twins; young adult twins; young twins
    "best friend" expectation for, 77–78, 85–86, 126
    bond between, 1, 15–16
    creating resilience in, 89
    decision-making and, 26–27
    individuation and, 14, 24, 27, 29–30, 65–66, 71–74, 157
    monoamniotic, 77
    self-reliance and, 63–64
    with special needs, 20–22
    stereotypic cultural expectations for, 2, 18, 25, 75–76, 126
    triangulation and, 67–68

websites, 159
Woodward, Joan, 135

young adult twins. *See also* intimate relationships
    caretaking behaviors and, 61–62
    codependency and, 79–80
    competitiveness between, 83–84
    differences between, 81–84
    emotional entitlement and, 69–70
    individuation and, 65–66, 71–74
    triangulation and, 67–68
young twins
    books for, 159
    caretaking syndrome and, 19
    comparisons between, 19
    decision-making and, 26–27
    differences between, 26–27
    dressing, 18
    friends and, 15–16, 24–25
    gift giving and, 10–12
    individuation and, 14, 24
    school and, 17–19, 23–25
    separating, 17, 18, 23–25
    with special needs, 20–22

About the Author

DR. JOAN A. FRIEDMAN is a gifted psychotherapist who has devoted many years of her professional career to educating twins and their families about twins' emotional needs. Having worked through her own twinship challenges and parented her fraternal twin sons, she is a definitive expert on twin development.

She is the author of *Emotionally Healthy Twins: A New Philosophy for Parenting Two Unique Children*, *The Same but Different: How Twins Can Live, Love, and Learn to Be Individuals*, and *Twins in Session: Case Histories in Treating Twinship Issues*. She has spoken to and consulted with culturally diverse groups of twins around the world. Dr. Friedman's work focuses on issues that adult twins confront as they adjust to life as singletons after having been raised as twins.

You can reach Dr. Friedman via

Website: www.joanafriedmanphd.com
Instagram: @dr.joanfriedmantwinexpert
Facebook: Joan A. Friedman, PhD - Twin Expert, Author, and Therapist
LinkedIn: Joan A. Friedman, Ph.D. Psychotherapist, Twin Expert, Author
X: @Joanafriedman